Thomas Reid's 'Inquiry'

D1531215

Thomas Reid

Thomas Reid's 'Inquiry'

The Geometry of Visibles and the Case for Realism

with a new Afterword

Norman Daniels

Foreword by Hilary Putnam

STANFORD UNIVERSITY PRESS
Stanford, California

Stanford University Press
Stanford, California

© 1974, 1989 by the Board of Trustees of the
Leland Stanford Junior University
Originally published 1974 by Burt Franklin & Co., Inc.

Printed in the United States of America

ISBN 0-8047-1504-1 (cl.)
0-8047-1712-5 (pbk.)

LC-88-60488

To My Parents

Table of Contents

Chapter V: Reid's Nativism

Acknowledgments

This essay is based on material included in my Ph.D. dissertation (Harvard, 1970), titled *Thomas Reid's Discovery of a Non-Euclidean Geometry: A Case Study in the Relation between Theory and Practice*. I am grateful to various fellow graduate students and friends for their helpful suggestions on that original material and especially to Professor W. V. O. Quine for his careful reading and kind encouragement. But to Professor Hilary Putnam, a friend as well as teacher, I owe my greatest thanks. Without his many hours of discussion, advice, reading and encouragement I would never have completed the original essay. He has continued to offer important suggestions in this revision. I am also indebted to Professor Dirk Struik for his suggestions covering the material in the first chapter, and to Professors Richard A. Watson, Hugo A. Bedau and Daniel C. Dennett, who have offered other helpful suggestions. Mrs. Carol Wharton was of considerable help in preparing the manuscript. The Philosophy of Science Association has kindly given me permission to use material in Chapter I from my article "Thomas Reid's Discovery of a Non-Euclidean Geometry" (*Philosophy of Science,* June 1972, 39: 219-234).

Finally, I would like to thank my parents and sister for their support and encouragement during the period of research and writing of the original essay, and my wife Anne for the many hours she has spent reading and discussing revisions with me with a view toward making the material more generally readable and available.

Foreword

Norman Daniels' lucid and carefully researched essay illuminates one of the most remarkable achievements of a philosopher who is one of the most profound students of the theory of knowledge up to the present time. Thomas Reid was certainly a genius; yet for many years his work was little known and his books were out of print. Today his work is coming into a modest vogue and new editions of the *Inquiry* and of both *Essays* have appeared. This new recognition of Reid comes for the most part from analytical philosophers who appreciate that Reid anticipated a number of highly contemporary ways of arguing. But such an appreciation, limited as it is to Reid as a forerunner of "ordinary language philosophy," is necessarily one-sided. To fully appreciate Reid, one must also appreciate his scientific genius and his deep roots in the scientific work of his time—especially the work being done in the theory of vision. The present book provides an easy and yet highly discerning access to Reid's accomplishments and to the context in which those accomplishments were made. At the same time, Norman Daniels gives a balanced evaluation of Reid's weaknesses as well as his strengths. Thus it seems to me likely that the present book will prove to be a fundamental source for all those who wish to make the acquaintance of one of the truly great epistemologists.

The history of philosophy is conventionally taught as a history of great men. But to understand the philosophical climate of an age it is necessary to know not only what the great philosophers were putting forward, but also to know what the average philosophy book or journal article contained, what the average philosophy teacher taught his classes, and so on. If we apply this criterion to the nineteenth century, and even to the early years of the twentieth century (up to World War I), we must be struck by a kind of philosophical unanimity on certain points that we rarely see today. All professional philosophers agreed, virtually without exception that no one ever sees a material object, that what we really see or directly see or immediately see are sense data or *impressions*. All professional philosophers, again virtually without exception, agreed that there was a theory called Naive Realism. This theory was supposed to hold that ordinary material objects—tables and chairs and so forth—are identical with *sensations*. This theory was not supposed to be believed by any philosopher; rather, philosophers believed that all people who were not philosophers, "common men," believed this theory. Not only was it believed that no one could *see* a material object; it was regarded as highly problematical whether anyone could conceive of a material object except as a sensation or some kind of mental construction out of sensations. Thus a fairly run-of-the-mill article by a philosopher of no great reputation appearing in an American journal, *The Journal of Philosophy,* about 1911, says quite confidently that all philosophers in the world are now idealists and that the only question left in philosophy is which version of idealism is going to triumph.

This amazing idealist consensus in philosophy of course fell apart after World War I. The impressive thing is that one epistemologist of the first rank opposed this consensus at its very origin and published incisive critiques of the arguments by Berkeley and Hume upon which this consensus came to be based. That epistemologist was Thomas Reid.

The character of the philosophy he was arguing against—of what was to become the philosophical consensus for the next century—was very clear to Reid. Thus he writes in the *Essays on the Intellectual Powers:* ". . . when we find the gravest philosophers, from Des Cartes down to Bishop Berkeley, mustering up arguments to prove the existence of a material world, and unable to find any that will bear examination; when we find Bishop Berkeley and Mr. Hume, the acutest metaphysicians of the age, maintaining that there is no such thing as matter in the universe—that sun, moon, and stars, the earth which we inhabit, our own bodies, and those of our friends, are only ideas in our minds, and have no existence but in thought; when we find the last maintaining that there is neither body nor mind—nothing in nature but ideas and impressions, without any substance on which they are impressed—that there is no certainty, nor indeed probability, even in mathematical axioms: I say, when we consider such extravagancies of many of the most acute writers on this subject, we may be apt to think the whole to be only a dream of fanciful men, who have entangled themselves in cobwebs spun out of their own brain. But we ought to consider that the more closely and ingeniously men reason from false principles, the more absurdities they will be led into; and when such absurdities help to bring to light the false principles from which they are drawn, they may be the more easily forgiven."

Part of Reid's strategy is to attack the claim that we only see sensations, and not material objects, and the claim that the common man is a "naive realist." It is in these destructive arguments that Reid resembles a contemporary analytical philosopher. But Reid is not satisfied with mere destruction.

Both Berkeley and Hume, in spite of many unclarities, seem to identify concepts more or less with mental images. If the concept of a chair is just the image of the chair, and the concept of a phenomenal chair (that is, of the image of a chair or the visual impression of a chair) is itself just an image, than it seems as if they must be the same. What difference can there be between the image of a chair and the image of an image of a chair? Of course, I am crudely simplifying an argument to which Berkeley gives an enormous amount of space, and which he elaborates in many subtle ways. But in essence I think the argument I have just given is the essential one. The essential point is that if concepts are images, then the claim that the concepts of phenomenal things and the concepts of physical things cannot be different is at least highly plausible. Thus it becomes incumbent upon every philosopher who seeks to refute Berkeley and Hume to propose a better theory of conceptualization than they had.

In our own day the search for an adequate theory of

conceptualization has occupied some of the greatest figures in analytical philosophy. In his last work, Carnap seemed to adopt a "network" theory of conceptualization. On this theory, to have a concept is the same thing as to know the role of a term in a certain network of scientific theory. This theory is of course overly narrow, since it confines conceptualization to the sphere of exact science. The later Wittgenstein put forward the theory that "meaning is use"; that is, that having a concept is not having an image, or a mental presentation of any kind, but rather having an ability, the ability to use words in the various "language games." This theory is of course not antithetical to Carnap's, as is often thought, but embraces Carnap's as a special case. Obviously the role of sensation concepts in either science or in ordinary language is very different from the role of thing concepts in either science or in ordinary language. Thus "role" or "use" theories of meaning are in no danger of confusing the concept of a thing with the concept of a sensation or of making it a mystery that we can have the concept of a thing as distinct from the concept of a sensation.

Some of the old idealist puzzles arise nonetheless. For one thing, any realist wants to maintain that the concepts we employ in science don't *merely* have a "use"; he wants to maintain that they *refer*. Realists believe that the sentences we utter in science and ordinary language are very often either true or false, and that what makes them true or false is something external. But in the later Wittgenstein, for example, talk about use seems to leave no room for talk about reference; indeed, Wittgenstein seems to dismiss the notion of reference in the opening pages of the *Philosophical Investigations* as "occult." The late Quine tries to give a theory of language which reconciles both a use theory of meaning with an account of reference and truth. But strange puzzles about "indeterminacy of translation" and "underdetermination" arise to leave us, apparently, in almost as bad a predicament as the idealists left us.

My own belief is that a functionalist theory of meaning and a realist account of reference and truth can be reconciled;

but there is clearly a great deal of philosophical work to be
done in this direction. The problem to which Reid was
addressing himself, then, is hardly one that we can regard as
having yet been solved. Reid, as we remarked, saw the need to
attack the theory of conceptualization associated with what
he called the Ideal System, and to replace it with something
better. He did not anticipate contemporary functionalist
accounts of conceptualization; but what he did come up with
was extremely interesting. In hundreds of pages of very careful
psychological and epistemological analysis, Reid tries to show
that conceptualization requires the use of abstract schemata,
and that these schemata can be in no way identified either with
images or with simple abstractions from images. These
abstract schemata are very close to the innate concepts that
Noam Chomsky has recently postulated. Certainly Reid's
concern with innate human cognitive structure is very closely
related to Chomsky's. Thus Reid tries to show that the
concept of extension, for example, is not derived from vision
as the empiricists thought. It is, on Reid's view, an innate
schema which we use to interpret both vision and touch. It is
in the context of carrying through this argument that Reid is
led to his amazing "premature" discovery of non-Euclidean
geometry.

   As just one facet of his very complex argument, Reid
raises the question: what geometry would we be led to if we
really did abstract geometry solely from vision? He argues
that the geometry of (monocular) vision is not Euclid's
geometry but another geometry which, he argues, is just as
consistent as Euclid's geometry although incompatible with
it. This geometry is the geometry that we today call
Riemannian geometry—although Reid was, of course,
writing decades before Riemann. Reid not only states a
number of theorems of this geometry—for example, that
every straight line has the same finite length—but proceeds to
give what we would today call an operational interpretation of
this geometry by the very modern technique of telling a
science fiction story about some beings he calls the
Idomenians. Reid's conclusion is that human beings impose

Euclidean geometry on the world, not because Euclid's geometry is the "geometry of the visibles," but in spite of the fact that it is *not* the geometry of the visibles.

   In an important chapter, Norman Daniels shows how both Berkeley and Reid assign to visual sense data what were in fact just the properties of images on the retina, and he shows that the virtual identification was made because scientific theory of vision at the time stopped with surface optics. This section of Daniels' book seems to be important for the understanding of all of traditional epistemology, not just Reid, and even for the understanding of a good deal of twentieth-century philosophy. Reid's argument against identifying what we perceive with the images on our retinas is an earlier version of what is today Chomsky's argument against Quine's notion of stimulus meaning. Quine today assumes that what a subject perceives can be read off in some way from the stimulations of his surface nerve endings—in the case of vision, this would be just from retinal images—whereas Chomsky, like Reid, argues that conceptualization plays such a large part in perception that there is no hope of determining what a person sees simply from what is on his retina or on his surface nerve endings.

   Given the incisiveness of Reid's critique of the Ideal System, the extraordinary depth and power of his analysis, the intrinsic interest of his positive theory, one may well wonder why Reid went so decisively out of fashion. A number of factors appear to have been responsible. Reid's philosophical successor was a man named William Hamilton (not to be confused with the mathematician of the same name). Hamilton was pompous, vain, and extraordinarily obtuse. Time and time again in reading Reid, one has to writhe at a footnote inserted by Hamilton (Hamilton was Reid's editor). Hamilton became known as *the* representative of Reid's school—the school of Scottish "common sense" philosophy. So when John Stuart Mill demolished Hamilton in a famous philosophical polemic, the entire school faded out of favor.

   But it would be unfair to put all the blame for Reid's philosophical demise on Hamilton. There were deep weaknesses in Reid's own philosophical thought—in particular what Daniels refers to as Reid's "dogmatism." For Reid, what was innate in human conceptual structure was also necessarily true—here Reid anticipates the central problem of Kantian philosophy. And Reid's followers, even more than Reid, tended to "solve" philosophical problems the easy way, by taking to be innate whatever they needed for their purposes—the existence of God, the immortality of the soul, free will, or whatever. It was just this dogmatic aspect of the school that Mill was to ridicule so effectively.

So, while Reid cannot be regarded as having possessed final solutions either to the problem of human conceptualization, or to the skeptical problems posed by the empiricists, he did "help to bring to light the false principles" from which the empiricists proceeded. And his work, and Norman Daniels' discussion of that work, should be of value to all who are interested in the problems of epistemology and cognitive psychology today.

Hilary Putnam

Harvard University
Fall 1973

Introduction

The Scotsmen Thomas Reid and David Hume were only a year apart in age, but the publication of Reid's first major work, *The Inquiry into the Human Mind* in 1764, twenty-five years after Hume's *Treatise on Human Nature*, marks the beginning of a new philosophical generation. It inaugurates a full-blown anti-skeptical, anti-idealist critique of Berkeley and Hume. Many of the main points in the *Inquiry* grew out of a weekly discussion group Reid had organized at Aberdeen, where he was a professor of philosophy. Members of this group later became known as the Scottish School of Common Sense and continued to put forward anti-empiricist views well into the 19th century.

Although Reid later develops the epistemological points of the *Inquiry* in his *Essays on the Intellectual Powers of Man* (1785) and applies them to moral philosophy in *Essays on the Active Powers of the Human Mind* (1788), in this essay we shall concern ourselves entirely with the *Inquiry*. There are several reasons for narrowing our focus to the *Inquiry*. First, Reid develops most of his main epistemological ideas in the *Inquiry*. The later works to a considerable extent, though by no means completely, contain elaborations, extensions, and applications of Reid's earlier ideas. A careful study of these developments warrants a separate, full-length investigation. Second, the presentation of Reid's ideas in the *Inquiry* is especially revealing because it shows more clearly than the later works Reid's active role as a participant in an experimentalist tradition trying to develop a science of the mind. But third, and most important for my purposes, it is in the *Inquiry* and not the later works that we find the body of scientific and philosophical problems that leads Reid to his startling discovery of a non-Euclidean geometry some sixty years before the mathematicians. By keeping the focus of my discussion on the setting of that discovery in the *Inquiry*, and by not digressing into subsequent developments, however interesting, I hope to show more clearly that Reid's discovery is no isolated freak but has real roots in his scientific tradition and in his defense of realism.

Reid's main purpose in the *Inquiry* is to show that a version of realism, reflecting our common sense belief in a material world, is compatible with the development of a true science of the human mind. To show this compatibility, Reid attacks the "Ideal System," the dominant 18th-century theory of mind whose development Reid traces from Descartes, through Malebranche and Locke, to its fuller articulation in Berkeley and Hume. On Reid's view, the Ideal System had wandered far from its original goal. It had been developed in order to explain how the human mind came to be affected by the world around it and acquired knowledge of that world, including knowledge of itself. But in its most developed form, it led to monstrous, skeptical conclusions—that there can be no material world which causes our sensations, that if there was such a world, we could have no knowledge of it, that the only objects of our knowledge are our ideas, and that we have no legitimate notion of mind as well. Reid argues that these skeptical and idealist conclusions are not simply the results of philosophical tricks or sophistical thinking, as some 18th-century contemporaries had thought. Rather they follow directly from basic principles of the Ideal System—especially its theory of concept formation—which therefore ought to be reassessed.

Reid fears that without such a major reassessment of the Ideal System, the credibility of any scientific approach to the study of the mind and senses is in jeopardy. Reid is directly affected by this threat. He views himself as a scientist participating in a broad experimentalist tradition that had been much influenced by Newton. Workers in this tradition—including not only prominent philosophers, but also physicists, physicians and clergymen—sought to reveal the objective laws that governed the working of the mind and body, just as Newton's laws revealed how God had organized the universe. In the Scottish schools of medicine at the time,

this experimental approach, with its explicit Newtonian
orientation, reigned supreme, in many cases under the
guidance of Continentally trained students of Boerhaave.
Hume's *Treatise* clearly shows this Newtonian influence.

The experimentalist orientation is especially clear in the
Inquiry. A full third of Reid's *Inquiry* is devoted to discussion
of actual and hypothetical (thought) experiments on various
phenomena—everything from distance discrimination to
squinting. As I show in Chapters II and V, Reid is conversant
with the very latest developments in 18th-century theory of
vision, from Berkeley through James Jurin and Robert Smith
to William Porterfield. Without a realist stance, Reid feels,
little sense can be made of this whole experimentalist
approach. To be sure, Reid repeatedly cites Newton's
warnings against drawing conclusions or speculating about
"causes" that lie deeper than the experimental phenomena
being studied. But it would be mistaken to think Reid takes
Newton's warning as an attack on "underlying" or "real"
causes. Rather, Reid mainly thinks this injunction rules out
only unwarranted speculation about the specific nature of
causal mechanisms "behind" the phenomena. For example,
in discussing certain problems in visual perception, he in-
vokes Newton's warning to remind us we have no knowledge
of *just how* sensations or impressions are transmitted. He
does not rule out our eventually finding out what the underlying mechanisms might be. The point here is that Reid
does think the material world and its various mechanisms are
"causes" which lie "deeper" than experimental phenomena.
This material world is God's creation, for Reid, and Newton's injunction is taken merely as a guide to insure we end
up understanding how it works. Reid stands opposed, then,
to Berkeley's phenomenalist reduction of science to the study
of mere regularities in our sense impressions or ideas. For
Reid, God works indirectly through matter—not directly at
the level of ideas, as for Berkeley—to produce regularities in
phenomena, and science tells us how that matter is organized
and works.

But why does Reid think the dominant 18th-century

theory of mind leads to skepticism and idealism? After all, the Ideal System itself seems to begin with a realist stance. Its original purpose is to explain how concepts are developed. And even its basic principles seem at first to be realist. For example, proponents of the Ideal System believe that if a concept, for example, the concept of red, is to apply to a feature of the world, then the concept must resemble the feature.[1] More exactly, a necessary condition for a person to have a concept that applies to a feature of the world is that he have a mental entity structured so that it bears a resembling relation to the feature of the world. The senses are taken to be the mechanism for achieving the necessary structuring of mental entities. To this theory of concept formation, Locke, Berkeley, and Hume add another "discovery" which undermines the initial realism, namely, that sensations cannot resemble features of the world ("nothing can be like an idea but an idea").

Especially in Berkeley's hands, these principles of the Ideal System lead to idealism in the following way. The principles tell us both that sensations cannot resemble real qualities of bodies and that we can have a concept of a real quality of bodies only if some sensations resembling that quality have produced the relevant concept in us. But, then, we can have a concept of a color only if that color is not a real quality of bodies. In other words, the concept of a given color does not, after all, apply to the external world. A similar argument applies to any purported concept of a real quality. As a result, the real world seems to fall out from under the concepts we thought applied to it. In order to reassure us against any sense of loss, Berkeley tries to convince us that terms like "color" always denote only sensations or "ideas" and not qualities, that we cannot lose what we never had. This is the point behind Berkeley's reassurance that everything remains "the same" after his reconstruction as before. The sensations or "ideas" become the "real" qualities.

Reid's attack on this kind of idealist move is discussed in detail in Chapter IV. The main point Reid makes is that our talk and beliefs about color can be explained only if we take

the term "color" to denote a real quality of bodies and not a
separate, mental sensation. Therefore, realism and not
idealism makes sense out of the way we think and talk about
bodies. We should not reject realism unless there is
overwhelmingly good reason to do so. Reid's attacks on the
Ideal System are an attempt to show there are no good reasons
for rejecting realism, at least none proposed in the Ideal
System.

Most of Reid's critique of the Ideal System is directed
against a "corollary" to the theory of concept formation, one
elevated to great importance by Hume: "to every quality and
attribute of body we know or can conceive, there should be a
sensation corresponding, which is the image and resemblance
of that quality."[2] This corollary has a dual function in the
Ideal System. On the one hand it is advanced as a testable
hypothesis asserting that sensations of a particular sort should
be found for every case of a concept applying to the external
world. On the other hand, once the corollary is proven, it can
be used as the basis for what Reid calls a "tribunal of
inquisition." Ideas (concepts) are tried before this tribunal to
determine if they have any real application to the external
world. Ideas for which there are no corresponding sensations
are "sentenced to pass out of existence, and to be, in all time to
come, an empty unmeaning sound, or the ghost of a departed
entity."[3]

Reid complains that the tribunal was used even though
no one had ever proved this theory of concept formation
true—including its famous corollary. Reid proposes a
"crucial test" intended to reveal a major set of counterexamples to it. The great bulk of argumentation in his central
chapters on "Touch" and "Seeing"—which I discuss in
Chapter IV—is devoted to showing that having sensations of
extension and figure is neither a necessary nor a sufficient
condition for having concepts of these important qualities. By
trying to reduce to a minimum, or to eliminate, the role of
introspectible sensations in concept formation, Reid hopes to
show that the Ideal System cannot be right in its conclusion
that our only objects of knowledge are our sensations or

relations among sensations. In other words, Reid primarily defends realism by showing that if we avoid the Ideal System's mistaken theory of concept formation, then we can avoid idealism.

One type of argument Reid uses is of central importance. He tries to show that our concepts of certain primary qualities are bound up in an elementary theory of bodies, a natively given primitive mechanics. Since the primitive mechanics gives us various ways of telling when and where these primary qualities are present, then we can develop and apply these concepts independently of our having all the corresponding sensations. The clearest example of such an argument is Reid's claim that a blind mathematician can acquire and apply the concept of visible figure without ever having any visual sensations. Given the real figure, magnitude and position of a body and an eye, we can use optical theory to deduce what the visible figure is. Simply set the eye in the center of a hollow sphere and project the real figure of the given body through the eye onto the sphere. Such a construction can readily be understood by a blind man knowing the appropriate mathematics. Similarly, the blind man can understand two further points. First, the distance between two visible points will vary with the magnitude of the angles the points subtend. And second, pure visual space is two-dimensional: the eye, until it is aided by experience, does not represent one object as nearer or more remote than another. In other words, the blind man can understand and apply a metric to a two-dimensional space which is a complete model for visual space. But then, Reid concludes, a blind man can have a clear and distinct conception of visible figure without ever having had any color sensation since he can "determine" using this model what the visible figure of something is. In addition, visible figures cannot be identical with visual sensations; nor can visible figures be abstractions solely from visual sensations.

This last argument not only adds to Reid's arsenal against the Ideal System's theory of concept formation, it contains, as well, Reid's most explicit formulation of an alternative analysis of what is involved in having a concept. According to Reid, proponents of the Ideal System believe a concept is a mental entity bearing structural resemblance either to sensations or to qualities of bodies.[4] The structural resemblance is needed to explain how the concept can apply either to sensations (Berkeley) or to real qualities (Locke). But as a result of Reid's arguments, there need be no sensation of visible figure at all. Clearly, then, no relation of resemblance can hold. So not only is the Ideal System's theory of concept formation threatened, but so too is its whole analysis of what concepts are and how they apply.

Reid's argument about the blind mathematician suggests we can tell that someone has a certain concept if we can find out whether or not he has a certain set of abilities. Given certain information, the blind mathematician is able to distinguish one visible figure from another, which Reid takes to be the central ability involved in having the concept of visible figure. The key to Reid's argument here—as in his similar proof that there are no special tactile sensations for primary qualities—is that the concept of visible figure is integrated into a body of mathematical and optical theory. One can know such a theory without having had sensations corresponding to each concept in the theory. Knowledge of the theory gives one a variety of abilities. If one can be shown to have the relevant abilities, then one has the concept in question. This directly undercuts Hume's thesis that every idea (concept) must have a corresponding sensation (our "corollary," above). And it undercuts Hume's use of this thesis in his "tribunal" in which he declares concepts illegitimate when we can find no corresponding sensations. Reid's appeal to the connection between having concepts and having certain abilities is not developed as a comprehensive alternative analysis for all concepts. At best, Reid has given an alternative only for visible figure and primary qualities revealed through touch, what we might call "theory bound" concepts (see Chapter IV, Sections 2,3).

It is worth trying to forestall an objection at this point. It might be thought that Reid is entitled to claim only that

the blind mathematician has a concept of figure, thought of
as an abstract set of relations, but he is not entitled to claim
this figure is specifically visual or tactual. Two points should
be noted, however. First, as I show in Chapter I and IV, visible and tactual figures have different geometries—so it cannot simply be the case that the blind mathematician is
abstracting a figure common to both modalities. But second,
and more in answer to the point, Reid would probably argue
that vision and touch reveal to us different *real* sets of
relations—e. g. figures—which are "real" even if they are in
some sense "abstract." We know what a given visible figure
is when we know what "set of relations" or figure vision
would reveal to us on a given occasion. And we can know
what the relevent figure is without the medium of vision, that
is, without visual sensations or impressions. Reid's argument
here is not an oversight—it is a position that assumes realism
in order to show we *can* make sense of it.

The central idea in Reid's argument about the blind
mathematician—that one can apply a metric to a two-
dimensional visible space—leads him to make a most startling
discovery. Some 60 years before the mathematicians, in
complete isolation from 18th-century work on the theory of
parallels, Reid uses this idea to develop a full-blown non-
Euclidean geometry, the "geometry of visibles." Reid constructs a special visible space, offers theorems of a doubly
elliptical geometry to describe its properties, and suggests the
surface of a sphere as a natural model for the geometry. Reid
is fully aware his geometry is a consistent alternative to
Euclid's, although, in contrast to Gauss and Lobachevsky,
he does not see the important new scientific and
philosophical problems his discovery implies. Perhaps Reid
fails to see these implications because he is primarily interested in using his discovery to defeat Berkeleyan idealism
about space. For example, Reid insists the new geometrical
objects, the visibles, are "real and external to the mind," and
are not just Berkeleyan sensations or appearances.

Reid's discovery of a non-Euclidean geometry, although
developed in isolation from 18th-century work in geometry,

did not just fall out of the sky. Here, too, a theoretical discovery is related to a body of scientific—albeit, non mathematical—practice. The "Geometry of Visibles" is not just an incidental chapter in the *Inquiry*. Any effort to explain how Reid came to make his discovery leads to all the central problems and arguments of the *Inquiry*. And it is just such an effort that lies behind the organization of this essay: Reid's discovery is discussed in detail in Chapter I; in each of Chapters II through IV, I relate some part of the origin of Reid's discovery to some central concern of the *Inquiry* as a whole.

In Chapter II, I explain why Reid thinks visual space is two-dimensional, one of the central technical features of Reid's geometry. But my discussion of the distance perception problem also shows the degree to which Reid views himself as a scientist whose central task is that of helping to develop a scientific theory of the mind. It shows in more detail just what kind of scientific practice Reid thinks is threatened by the skepticism and the idealism of the Ideal System.

In Chapter III, I show that Reid develops his geometry of the visibles as a specific reply to Berkeley's arguments about visual space in *Essay Toward A New Theory of Vision*. In this early work, Berkeley argues that visual space, in contrast to tangible space, is really "in the mind" and cannot be an object of geometrical study. Reid wants to show that visibles are just as legitimate an object of geometrical study as tangibles, and therefore, that both are equally "real and external to the mind." Finally, in Chapter IV, I discuss in some detail Reid's analysis of the Ideal System and his arguments attacking its theory of concept formation. As I show, it is one of these central arguments, the argument about the blind mathematician, that contains the kernel of Reid's discovery.

In Chapter V, I discuss Reid's nativist alternative to the Ideal System's theory of concept formation. I show that Reid's nativism, as well as his geometry, has roots in working problems in 18th-century theory of vision, and I discuss problems with Reid's appeal to nativism in that context. In

particular, I show that the nativist hypothesis was advanced
whenever existing learning theory could not account for a
given phenomenon. But the main point of my discussion is to
show that Reid offers a broad theory of unrevisable beliefs
which are "parts of our constitution." For example, Reid
equips us natively with mathematical axioms, the ability to see
necessary relations among things and to carry out deductions,
and the disposition to form particular mathematical motions
of points, lines, figures, and dimensionality when exposed to
certain sensory inputs. The effect in this case is that Euclidean
propositions are synthetic *a priori* for tangible (real) space and
the theorems from the geometry of visibles are synthetic *a
priori* for visible space.

Reid's philosophy of geometry is only part of a more
general theory of unrevisability. Reid also uses his nativism to
protect us from birth against skepticism and idealism. Not
only do we have given to us from birth certain inductive
abilities—the abilities to trace particular facts to general rules,
to observe the connections among events, and to search for
causes—but also we are given natively a belief in the principle
of the uniformity of nature. In this way, Reid rather
dogmatically "solves" Hume's puzzle about induction, that
we have no way of justifying our beliefs that the future will
resemble the past. For Reid, if the belief in uniformity is false,
then we are deceived by the God who made us and there is no
remedy. Similarly, Reid builds into us the concept of external
existing things and events, as well as an unshakable belief in
their externality and existence. In other words, realism is built
into our constitution on a foundation of innate ideas—this is
"common sense" realism. In addition, we are natively
disposed to have confidence in the testimony of our senses and
memory—a view which foreshadows certain contemporary
efforts to give *prima facie* credence to sense testimony.

These various anti-skeptical abilities, dispositions, and
beliefs are among those Reid groups together as "common
sense." Common sense puts us under a necessity to form
certain concepts and to hold certain beliefs. It provides us with
fixed, unrevisable points in our theories. Reid seems to believe

that "by our constitution" we are restricted *both* to having certain fixed, unrevisable points in our theories about the world *and* to having only experience compatible with those fixed points.

In what sense are these beliefs unrevisable? For one thing we are under a necessity to assent to them. We are so constructed that no one can really believe they are false unless they suffer from some form of insanity. More importantly, Reid thinks that it is impossible for us to do without these natively given concepts and beliefs. He offers two arguments: first, we can carry out no reasoning without using these principles as starting points, and second, we cannot act on beliefs that are contrary to common sense. This last argument is quite important. It amounts to the claim that beliefs must be related to practice, to action. Reid is insisting that skeptical beliefs cannot be acted on in practice and so must be rejected.

A real weakness of Reid's position is that the very point he makes in opposition to the skeptic is a point which raises a serious question about his own theory of unrevisability. If practice is the test of beliefs, then what is Reid's argument that practice can never force us to revise conceptions and beliefs we have "by our constitution"? And if practice is appealed to in order to reject skeptical beliefs, then why is God needed to guarantee that our natively given beliefs are true? These problems are taken up in Chapter V. Both in his appeal to God and in his appeal to nativism, Reid ends up saving realism through dogmatism. Reid's failure to provide a positive alternative to the Ideal System led many to forget that his battle against 18th-century idealism contained many victories.

Thomas Reid's 'Inquiry'

Chapter I:

The Geometry of Visibles

1. *The Non-Euclidean Geometry of Visibles*

In the chapter "The Geometry of Visibles" in *Inquiry into the Human Mind*, Thomas Reid constructs a special visible space, develops a doubly elliptical geometry for this space, and offers a natural model for the geometry, the surface of the sphere.[1]

At first sight, one assumes Reid could be doing no such thing in 1764 when *Inquiry* was published. He was not, after all, a geometer working on the theory of parallels, like the acknowledged 18th-century forerunners of non-Euclidean geometry. In spite of Reid's early interest in geometry, it is highly unlikely that he ever saw Gerolamo Saccheri's work[2] *Inquiry* was published two years before Johann Lambert's *Theorie der Parallel-Linien* (1766). He makes no remarks about the status of the parallels postulate. He does not introduce the theorems of his geometry as part of an effort to show that the fifth postulate could be derived from Euclid's other axioms. That is, he does not replace the parallels postulate with its negation (or the equivalent) and carry out systematic deductions, hoping to turn up a contradiction. In short Reid is not at all concerned with the body of mathematical practice that led Gauss, Lobachevsky, Bolyai and others to the major theoretical discovery that there is more than one consistent geometry.

Because we all believe that theory is related to practice and that ideas do not drop from the sky, Reid's divorce from any relevant mathematical tradition seems to leave us with these choices:

(1) Reid has *not* discovered a non-Euclidean geometry but is really offering his geometry of visibles simply as a

spherical geometry applicable to curved lines in Euclidean space.

ʌ)   (2) Reid *has* discovered a non-Euclidean geometry, but it is something of a theoretical scandal, born without benefit of any marriage between theory and practice.

ϡ)   (3) Reid *has* discovered a non-Euclidean geometry but its origins lie in a nonmathematical body of philosophical and scientific practice.

        The very fact that Reid was not a mathematician makes the first choice seem plausible. Spherical geometries were well known at the time.[3] Further, Reid seems hardly to intend anything very startling, since he hopes that the "mathematical reader" will follow him with "perfect facility."[4] What is more, Reid never questions whether or not Euclidean geometry is true of real space, and so he does not seem to be offering a full, competing alternative to Euclidean geometry.

        Nevertheless, in this Chapter I argue that this first choice is wrong and that Reid has indeed discovered a non-Euclidean geometry. The details of Reid's presentation of his geometry are contained in this section of Chapter I. In Section 2, I discuss what these new geometrical objects—the visibles—are. Reid believes that the visibles are "real" and "external to the mind." He thinks that his demonstration that we can study these objects mathematically is a strong argument against Berkeley's idealist treatment of visual space in *New Theory of Vision*. Finally, in Section 3, I contrast Reid's lack of awareness of the importance of his discovery with Gauss' and Lobachevsky's insights into the new problems implied by their discovery. In Chapters II through IV I prove that Reid's discovery grew out of both his interest in 18th-century theory of vision and his primary aim in the *Inquiry* to attack the dominant 18th-century theory of mind, the Ideal System.

        Reid presents his "geometry of visibles" in the following four steps:

        1) He refers the reader to standard definitions of basic notions, such as point, line, angle, etc.

        2) He uses these basic notions, plus an idealized eye with

special properties, to give an operationally defined visible space. He thus specifies operationally a model for his later theorems.

3) He claims that this visible space is "represented" by an arbitrary sphere encompassing the space. We can consider this step a relative consistency proof.

4) He offers some central theorems of the geometry, adapted from spherical geometry in an obvious way.

It is useful to discuss each step in turn, drawing as well on points made outside the chapter, "Geometry of Visibles," for purposes of elucidation.

The first step is rather simple. Reid defines 'point,' (*A*) 'line,' 'right line,' 'angle,' and 'circle,' "as in common geometry."[5] If we look for appropriate definitions in a contemporary *Euclid's Elements*, we find that Reid's definitions do no more than take these notions as primitive. For example,

  I. A Point is that which hath no Parts, or Magnitude.
  II. A Line is Length, without Breadth.
  III. The Ends (or Bounds) of a Line, are Points.
  IV. A Right Line, is that which lieth evenly between its
      Points.[6]

Of course, "between" is not defined. In a later discussion Reid tells us that a being who can conceive of three dimensions has a more "determined" notion of point, 'right line,' or surface than a being who can conceive of only two dimensions.[7] For example, 'right lines' "lie evenly" between end points in two dimensions for us, but only in one dimension for a being who does not conceive of depth. Different classes of lines are picked out as "right lines" by the two beings. Definition IV, then, does not seem to pick out a determinate class of lines unless we are told more about how it is to be used. Presumably, this problem does not normally arise because it is we who use the notion "right line."

The second step of Reid's presentation tells how to use (*2*) the basic notions to pick out a determinate class of objects, the visibles. Reid's eight "evident principles" provide a set of operational definitions which enable us to construct visible space. In effect, we are given an operationally specified model for the theorems Reid later offers, which is to say, a demonstration of the consistency of the geometry of visibles. For example, the first principle tells us how to apply our definition of "right line" so that we pick out a determinate class of visible right lines:

> Supposing the eye placed in the center of a sphere, every great circle of the sphere will have the same appearance to the eye as if it was a straight line. For the curvature of the circle being turned directly toward the eye, is not perceived by it. And for the same reason, any line which is drawn in the plane of a great circle . . . whether it be in reality [in real or tangible (Euclidean) space] straight or curve, will appear straight to the eye.[8]

It is necessary to sort out in some detail the features of Reid's construction. His own presentation is clear on at least these points:

a) the construction uses a single eye, and so we are building monocular visual space;

b) the eye is incapable of making any depth discrimination;

c) the sphere surrounding the eye can be arbitrarily large. He seems to be committed as well to the following specifications:

d) the eye retains normal field of vision when pointed in any direction;

e) the eye is capable of 360° rotation, but not translation.

One very important feature, the method of determining the length of visible lines, is not discussed in the course of Reid's eight "evident principles." In an earlier chapter, "Of Visible Figure and Extension," Reid introduces the relation "position with regard to the eye" (to which I return below). We can use this relation to obtain a measure of difference of position. The angle formed at the center (focal point) of the eye by rays projected from points having different positions with regard to the eye is a measure of difference of position: "this difference of position is greater or less in proportion to the angle made at the eye by the right line mentioned."[9] It is safe to assume that Reid intends this method of determining distance between points to be a feature of the construction in "Geometry of Visibles." Specifically,

f) if (d) and (e) are retained as features of the construction, then in order to measure distance between the positions of points, the eye must keep track of (1) angles formed by rays projected from points to the center of the stable (non-rotating) eye and (2) angle of rotation.

The abilities ascribed to the eye in point (f) operationally specify a metric for visible space. The metric is isomorphic to the metric for a unit sphere, and so it obviously satisfies the standard axioms for "distance." The metric Reid provides in point (f) should count as a direct refutation of Berkeley's claim in *New Theory of Vision* that visible extension is of "no constant, determinate magnitude."[10] Also, the provision of a metric should make it clear that Reid is not just concerned with a projective geometry in his geometry of visibles.

Alternative ways of measuring angles might require modification or abandonment of (d) and (e) and a consequently greater exercise of imagination in order for us to "see" with the modified eye. Since (f) suffices and is close to what Reid says, I accept it.

One final point is really corollary to the requirement (b), that the eye of the construction make no depth discriminations. Let us suppose that a rigid sheet of paper is suspended before the eye so that it can be seen distinctly at one view and such that the four corners are equidistant from the focal point (or center) of the eye. Midpoints of the sides are closer to the center of the eye than the corners but the eye does not see such differences. One way to construe the claim that the eye sees no such differences is to imagine that all points on the four edges (on the whole surface) appear equidistant to the eye of the construction. But this claim is equivalent (with an important qualification) to assuming that all points the eye sees appear as they would if they were projected onto an arbitrary sphere with the eye at its center. We can express this point in (g), which makes explicit the connection between (b) and (c) and which is of importance in understanding step three of Reid's presentation:

g) the eye sees all points in its visual field as (if they were) equidistant.

Actually, we can treat (g) as a guide to our imagination, aiding us in "seeing" through the eye of the construction: to imagine vision in which no depth discrimination is made, imagine seeing only points which are equidistant from the eye. But if the guide is not to mislead us, we must keep in mind one important qualification. We must withhold the judgment we, with ordinary vision, might be able to make—that a surface all of whose visible points are equidistant from the eye is curved. Reid argues that such a judgment involves discriminations in a third dimension; consequently, visible surfaces are neither curved nor plane.

Reid seems to think he is giving a model for human visual space. We have a choice: either we can take visual space constructed by use of (a)-(g) as a (drastic) idealization of human visual space, or we can treat it as a special, hypothetical visual space. Such an idealization, one of the goals of 18th-century theory of vision, is an approximation of what the "eye alone can see," without regard to deeper processes that coordinate vision and touch.[11] Each alternative is compatible with the claim that Reid is constructing a model for his non-Euclidean geometry.

The construction of visible space, and of lines and figures in it, is accomplished by a thought experiment: we are to imagine objects seen through an eye conforming to requirements (a)-(g). I call such an eye "The Eye". Let us engage in this experiment for a moment; then,

> every visible right line will appear to coincide with some great circle of the sphere; and the circumference of that great circle, even when it is produced until it returns into itself, will appear to be a continuation of the same visible right line, all the parts of it being visibly *in directum*.[12]

In Reid's construction, an eye incapable of translation, but free to rotate, has no way of seeing continuous extension of a

right line segment except by requiring the right line to return⌐
to itself. Imagine, for example, an infinitely (or
indeterminately) long wire stretched out straight in Euclidean
space, so that it forms a chord of a plane of an arbitrarily large
great circle with The Eye at the center of the great circle. What
The Eye would see, the visible figure of such a wire, is a
bounded line segment requiring at most 180° rotation for
complete viewing. But such a visible figure has not been
extended "as far as it may be continued," for that would imply
its occupation of 360° of visible space. Reid here seems to
offer (the modern reader) an operational definition of the
unbounded finitude of the (visible) right line for a space of
constant positive curvature. Actually, however, Reid speaks
of an "infinite" right line returning to itself.[13]

In Reid's "evident principles" 4-8, the remainder of the
second step of his presentation, he gives operational
specifications for "angle," "right-lined triangle," "circle,"
"visible figure" and "visible space." These principles function
in the same way as the first ones. They tell us how our basic
notions are used to pick out a determinate class of objects,
the visibles.

In the Third Step of Reid's presentation, also contained
in the eight "evident principles," Reid discusses the relation
between visibles and their projections onto an arbitrarily large
sphere encompassing The Eye. Reid argues that the
projections onto a sphere *represent* visible figures.[14] In the
third principle he says:

> [E]very visible right line, when it is continued *in directum,*
> as far as it may be continued, will be *represented* by a
> great circle of a sphere, in whose center the eye is placed.
> (emphasis added)[15]

Similarly, "the whole surface of the sphere will represent the
whole of visible space," and "every visible figure will be
represented by that part of the surface of the sphere, on which
it might be projected, the eye being in the center."[16]

The fact that projections on a sphere "represent" the
visibles is centrally important to Reid. It provides him with an

easy way of specifying the mathematical properties of visibles.
For example in "evident principles" 4 and 5, Reid reads off
obvious mathematical properties of the visibles from their
analogues in the model:

> [S]ince the visible lines appear to coincide with the great
> circles, the visible angle comprehended under the former,
> must be equal to the visible angle comprehended under
> the latter. But the visible angle comprehended under the
> two great circles, when seen from the center, is of the
> same magnitude with the spherical angle which they
> really comprehend, as mathematicians know; therefore
> the visible angle made by any two visible [right] lines, is
> equal to the spherical angle made by the two great circles
> of the sphere which are their representatives.

Similarly, in principle 5, he argues that a visible right-lined
triangle will,

> coincide in all its parts with some spherical triangle . . .
> to the eye they will be one and the same, and have the
> same mathematical properties. The properties therefore
> of visible right-lined triangles, are not the same with the
> properties of plain triangles, but are the same with those
> of spherical triangles.[17]

In effect, by providing us with a natural model for his
geometry, Reid is giving a relative consistency proof: the
geometry of visibles is consistent if spherical geometry is.

But what considerations led Reid to single out the sphere
to represent visible space? The anatomy of the human eye
seems to have been one motivating consideration. As I show
in the next Section, Reid believes that the material impression
on the retina "suggests" visible figure. At one point he says
that the visible figure of a body is "the same figure [as] that
which is projected upon the *tunica retina* in vision."[18] Since the
material impression on the retina is what "suggests" visible
figure, Reid seems to feel we can preserve the properties of
visible figure if we preserve the properties of the material
impression.[19] But the retina is treated by Reid as just a portion
of the surface of a hollow sphere. To preserve properties of a

material impression on such a surface, Reid projects the impression back through the center (focal point) of The Eye and out onto an arbitrary sphere. Since distinct points of the impression are equidistant from the center of The Eye, we must project them equidistantly, i.e., onto an arbitrarily large sphere whose center is the center of the eye. In effect, these are symmetry and simplicity considerations which rest on anatomical features of the eye and accord with properties (d), (e), and (f) of The Eye.

Property (b) of The Eye plays a key role here as well. The inability of the eye to make depth discriminations is what collapses the equivalence relation, "having the same position with regard to The Eye," into an identity relation for The Eye. Further, property (g) has its effect. Property (g) is supposed to guide our imagination in seeing through The Eye. It tells us to imagine that seeing no depth differences between visible points is just like seeing all visible points equidistant from the eye. But this is equivalent to projecting visible points onto an arbitrary sphere.

Anatomical considerations and Reid's theory of perception, as well as the special properties of The Eye make the sphere the "natural" representation of visible space. Projection onto no other surface preserves the properties of visible figure. Projection onto a cube with The Eye at its center would violate the symmetry considerations based on the anatomy of the eye (a sphere, in Reid's idealization). Similarly, it would seem arbitrary in view of property (g), the claim that The Eye sees all points as (if they are) equidistant. In view of these considerations, Reid feels justified in using the sphere as a model for the visibles.

It is worth a reminder at this point that the Euclidean sphere is only a model for the visible space we construct using The Eye in our thought experiment. It would be wrong to think that since such a central place is given to projections onto a sphere, and since at one point Reid says, "This projection is the visible figure he [the blind mathematician] wants,"[20] then the geometry of visibles is really nothing more than the geometry of curved lines in Euclidean space. It would be wrong to think that Reid is not concerned with a special space and its non-Euclidean geometry. Such an interpretation cannot be right for many reasons already discussed. It overlooks, for example, Reid's own claim that the sphere only "represents" visible space. Of course we (but not The Eye) can use the sphere as a Euclidean model of visible space since we normally have a "conception" of three-dimensional real space. We simply interpret a (visible) right line to be a great circle (a curved line), a right-lined triangle to be a spherical triangle (a curved surface), and so on. To The Eye, however, a right line (segment) is the same visible object as a (segment of a) great circle; it stands in the same position with regard to The Eye. The Eye does not distinguish, as we can, the curved great circle segment from its straight chord. A segment of a great circle "lieth evenly" between its end points and so is a visible right line. Similarly, as is pointed out in the discussion of (g) above, a visible right-lined triangle is neither plane nor curved, since The Eye can make no such distinction. In constructing visible space by our thought experiment using The Eye, we are restricted to distinctions The Eye can make. The geometry of visibles cannot be just the geometry of curved lines in Euclidean space.

In the fourth and final step of his presentation, Reid lists sample theorems from the geometry of visibles. Among his specimen propositions are:

 3. A right line returning into itself, divides the whole of visible space into two equal parts, which will both be comprehended under this right line.

 6. If two lines be parallel, that is, every where equally distant from each other, they cannot both be straight.

 9. Right-lined triangles that are similar, are also equal.

 10. Of every right-lined triangle, the three angles taken together, are greater than two right angles.

 12. Unequal circles are not as the squares of their diameters, nor are their circumferences in the ratio of their diameters.[21]

It is clear, especially from what he says in "evident principles" 4 and 5, that he is adapting his theorems in an obvious way from spherical geometry. That is, he replaces the standard Euclidean terms (and their standard interpretation) "great circle," "spherical angle," "spherical triangle," and "(spherical) circle," by his operationally specified (and interpreted) terms "visible right-line," "visible angle," and so forth.

Most importantly, Reid claims that the resulting "propositions with regard to visible figure and space, which we offer only as a specimen, may be mathematically demonstrated" from the "evident principles,"—"*and are not less true nor less evident than the propositions of Euclid, with regard to tangible figures.*" (emphasis added)[22]

> [These propositions] demonstrate . . . that those figures and that extension which are the immediate objects of sight, are not the figures and the extension about which common geometry is employed . . . that . . . a figure presented to [the] eye . . . is only a sign and representative of a tangible figure . . . and that these two figures have different properties, so that what (the mathematician) demonstrates of the one, is not true of the other.[23]

There can remain little doubt that Reid intends the geometry of visibles to be an alternative to Euclidean geometry, although he never intends it to be a competing geometry for real space.

Thus, for example, Reid's doubly elliptical space (proposition 3) contains *no parallel straight lines* (proposition 6), where "parallel" is defined by equidistance rather than by sharing a perpendicular with another given line. The Eye, placed in a sphere with North and South Poles, will see the equator to be parallel to all other latitude demarcations; but the latter, not being geodesics, are not seen as right lines by The Eye, but as circles.

The non-Euclidean propositions of Reid's fourth step are, then, propositions true of a space which we can construct by undertaking the thought experiment demanded in Step Two. Step Two tells us how to interpret the basic terms of the geometry by telling us how to pick out a special set of geometrical objects, the visibles. So, Step Two gives us an operationally specified model for the theorems of the geometry of visibles (what we might call an "experiential" consistency proof since we construct the visibles by experiencing the work through The Eye). Step Three gave us a "natural" Euclidean model for the non-Euclidean geometry of visibles—and so a relative consistency proof.

Reid feels obliged to explain why no one had ever discovered the geometry of visibles before him. After all, how can we explain why geometers have made such a systematic oversight for over "twenty centuries"?[24] To be sure, according to Reid's theory of mind, we are "inattentive" to visible figure, always treating it as a sign for tangible figure.[25] But shouldn't geometers have detected some error in their calculations or measurements? Reid answers this question with the following argument:

1) a small part of a spherical surface differs not sensibly from a plain surface.

2) the human eye is so formed that an object which is seen distinctly and at one view can occupy but a small part of visible space.

3) [Therefore], plain figures which are seen at one view, when their planes are not oblique but direct to the eye, differ little from the visible figures which they present to the eye.[26]

Reid's explanation shows that he wants our construction, using properties (a)-(g) of the eye, to be taken as an idealization of human visual space, not as a construction of some hypothetical, special space (see Chapter Two). Of course, only the interpretation as an idealization accounts for the appearance of Reid's geometry in the *Inquiry* since he is trying to explain features of human experience and knowledge. He is, after all, not a geometrician, but rather a cognitive psychologist of the eighteenth century.

2. *The Nature of the Visibles*

It will be helpful to say at this point what sorts of objects the visibles are. We may begin by trying to establish what kinds of entities they are *not*. Are we committed, for example, in quantifying over visible points and lines, to the existence of such entities as "looks" or "appearances" or "visual images?" Is the geometry of visibles a "phenomenal" geometry, a theory giving the properties of such entities?

Although Reid is not unhappy about admitting sensations or impressions to his universe, the whole thrust of his realism seems to go against collapsing a visible figure into a visual image, some "picture in the head." In fact, Reid is quite explicit—visible figure is *not* a sensation, *nor* does it "resemble" a sensation. He does not even claim visible figure is "suggested" by a sensation, where by "sensation" he means something of which we are conscious. Rather, it is "suggested" by the "material impression" upon the retina; and we are not conscious of material impressions on the retina.[27] (I return later to Reid's remark about the retina, for it is revealing of the motivation behind Reid's construction.)

But if visible figure is not something in the head, then what is it? Before I attempt a realist account of visible figure, it will help to see how Reid handles tangible figure, since he claims, "the visual figure of bodies is a real and external object to the eye, as their tangible figure is to the touch."[28] Unfortunately, Reid makes no explicit distinction between "tangible figure" and "real figure." Since he also claims that our knowledge of real figure is arrived at through touch, the conflation is seen to be not so harmful as it might first appear, especially if we remember that tangible figure, like visible figure, neither is nor "resembles" a sensation. It, too, is not some entity in the head.

The real figure of a body is the array of its extreme or boundary points in real space, "the situation of its several parts with regard to one another."[29] Two features of Reid's theory of perception seem to underlie the conflation of real and tangible figure, on the one hand, and their difference from visible figure on the other. The first feature is Reid's claim that tangible or visible figure is "suggested" to us by "material impressions" on organs of touch or the retina. A tangible point is a real point in space (a part of a real body) having the "power" to produce a material impression on one's hand. For a tangible point to make an impression, it must be in contact with the organ of touch—and this common sense fact could be what leads Reid to equate position in real space and position in tangible space. A cognitive psychologist like Reid might bring this point out by asking one to imagine that touch could have been different in the following way: rather than an impression being made by contact, touch would operate at a distance like vision, say by touch fibers being extremely sensitive to slight differences in gravitational fields. Then tangible and real points could not be so readily identified and touch would be much like vision.

A second feature of importance is that "by our constitution" we are given a "conception" of three dimensions for tangible space (and "so" for real space), but a conception of only two dimensions for visual space. A series of investigations by an organ of touch results in a series of material impressions. Perhaps these are formed into a composite, three-dimensional impression which in turn "suggests" the tangible figure. At any rate, we have a "conception" of three dimensions which permits material impressions of touch to "suggest" three-dimensional, Euclidean tangible figures. But such figures are congruent with all the boundary points of the real figure by an elaboration of the argument identifying tangible points and real points. For example, the real figure of my pen is a solid ellipse. The tangible figure revealed in exploring the pen with my hand is also a solid ellipse.

These two features of Reid's theory of perception begin with a realist view of space and objects in it. The conflation of real and tangible figure, given that theory of perception, is not a disastrous oversight, forcing Reid into some form of idealism.

The same two features of Reid's theory of perception

that lead to conflating tangible with real figure also lead to distinguishing both from visible figure. Consider the second feature first and the example of my pen. No composite visible figure can be constructed or "suggested", Reid might maintain, since three-dimensionality is not given "by our constitution" for visual space. Rather, if The Eye explores my pen, it sees only a sequence of visible figures: one may be an ellipse, another a circle with a point at its center.

Similarly, the first feature—that visible figure is "suggested" to us by the "material impression" on the retina—leads us to distinguish tangible from visible figure. Since the material impression of touch is made through direct contact with the body, it seems plausible to identify the positions of real and tangible points. When the material impression on the retina suggests a visible point, however, The Eye can pick out only an equivalence class of real points, since The Eye can make no depth discriminations. Reid explicitly introduces the appropriate relation *same position with regard to The Eye* as follows:

> Objects that lie in the same right line drawn from the center of the eye, have the same position, however different their distances from the eye may be: but objects which lie in different right lines drawn from the eye's center, have a different position; and this difference of position is greater or less, in proportion to the angle made at the eye by the right lines mentioned.[30]

Only those (boundary) points of the real figure which have different positions with regard to The Eye can affect the "material impression" and so be part of the visible figure. "[A]s the real figure of a body consists in the situation of its several parts with regard to one another, so its visible figure consists in the position of its several parts with regard to the eye."[31]

We can now say what sorts of entities the visibles are. Visible points, lines, and figures can be thought of as the objects that result when Reid's equivalence-relation, *same position with regard to The Eye*, is treated as an identity relation (for The Eye in the construction). Seeing through The Eye forces us to collapse the equivalence relation into an identity relation. When interpreting basic notions like point, line, and right line in order to construct visible space, we are always restricted to the determinations The Eye can make. Objects that have the same positions with regard to The Eye will be the same visible objects. This now gives us a way of restating the sense in which the notions of point, line, figure, and surface are "less determined" for a being that (having vision as its only sense) cannot conceive of three dimensions: the equivalence relation collapses into an identity relation.

There are some problems with this interpretation of Reid's visibles. So far we cannot identify a visible point with a particular real point, but only with an equivalence class of real points. Does this mean that we see equivalence classes of real points? Or is there a way to pick an obvious member of such an equivalence class and identify it as the real point which we see? Let us suppose we can pick the real point which, by an elaboration of Reid's causal theory, actually affects the retina and thus "suggests" the visible point. But if we do this for each real point of a body whose visible figure The Eye sees, then we have a problem: the array of those real points in real space is Euclidean (for Reid). But then that array cannot be identical with the visible figure, whose properties are non-Euclidean. Alternatively, we can project each real point in the causally specified array onto some arbitrary sphere with The Eye at its center. Can we identify the visible points of the visible figure with this array of real points in real space? No, once again, the transitivity of identity forces the points on the (Euclidean) sphere to have a non-Euclidean geometry or the visible figure to have a Euclidean geometry. We shall see in a moment that Reid does not *identify* visible figure with its projection onto a sphere, but claims only that such a projection *represents* visible figure. There is no easy way around Reid's predicament: when we see a visible point, we are seeing an equivalence class of real points.

We might say that the visible point is an "hypostatized" object. The Eye converts the equivalence class into an object, a visible point, which is the object we see when we see a visible point by means of The Eye. It is these objects, and not their projections onto a sphere, which are the visibles. Reid's geometry of visibles is developed in order to give a mathematical description of the properties of these special objects.

Are these special, hypostatized objects "real"? In many senses they clearly are. One can distinguish real visibles from imaginary ones—for example from visibles we might imagine to have Euclidean properties if the eye could "see distance." Similarly, they are not just fictitious objects of vision known only to the fictitious Idomenians, Reid's 18th-century version of the Flatmen.[32] Rather, the visibles are found in our own pure visual experience. Similarly, they are not just illusions or hallucinations. The visibles and their properties can be described and distinguished intersubjectively. They are not just subjective phenomena—a blind man can corroborate a description of the visible figure of a given object even though his private mental presentations are nothing like ours. Unlike imaginings, the visibles are not just products of acts of the mind. Visibles are there to be attended to in various ways. They are not brought into existence by each act of attending.

But Reid intends more than just these senses of "real". His main goal is to answer Berkeley's claim in *New Theory of Vision* that visible space is "in the mind" and tangible space is "external" to the mind. His arguments about the visibles are intended to show that nothing in Berkeley's actual arguments really challenges a consistent realist stance with regard to both tangible and visible space. For example, we can ask whether these hypostatized objects, the visibles, aren't really more "abstract" than real or tangible points, lines and figures. Reid can answer that they are equally "abstract," but nonetheless equally real and "external to the mind." Are these hypostatized objects "mental constructions," and so "in the mind" rather than "external to the eye"? Reid can answer that even if one thinks of these objects as constructions, still there can be little reason to place them "in the mind," since they are not constructions made up of sensations. In Chapter III, I show further how Reid uses his visibles and their geometry to reply to Berkeley's idealism with regard to visual space.

3. *Reid, Gauss, and Lobachevsky on the Significance of their Discoveries*

Although Reid very clearly sees that he has discovered a geometry distinct from the "common" or Euclidean geometry, he does not realize that this discovery raises new, important questions for science and the philosophy of science. He does remark that his fantasy creatures, the touchless Idomenians who use his two-dimensional visible geometry, will have to have a different physics and metaphysics from ours:

> [E]very Idomenian firmly believes that two or more bodies may exist in the same place . . . They often see two bodies meet, and coincide in the same place, and separate again, without having undergone any change in their sensible qualities by this penetration. When two bodies meet, and occupy the same place, commonly only one appears in that place, and the other disappears. That which continues to appear is said to overcome, the other to be overcome.[33]

But these somewhat whimsical observations are completely different from the very profound awareness of new scientific and philosophical problems on the part of the mathematicians, like Carl Friedrich Gauss and Nicholai Lobachevsky, when they began to realize they had discovered an alternative geometry.

Gauss, for example, very clearly treats his alternative geometry as a theory about real space. Its theorems are taken to describe features which—however counter-intuitive—will be observable if the theory is true. For example, he remarks in a letter to Taurinus (8 November, 1824):

> Should the non-Euclidean geometry be the true one, and that constant proportionality be of such magnitude that it lies in the region of our measurements on earth or in the heavens, then it can be ascertained *a priori*.[34]

Gauss, it seems, was aware that direct measurement may not be decisive because we may not know if we are measuring a sufficiently large portion of space.

Gauss also sees that new philosophical problems arise from his discovery. In particular, he views the very possibility of his new geometry being true as a challenge to philosophical theories, like Kant's, that treat geometry as comprised of *a priori* truths:

> I come even more to the conviction that the necessity of our geometry can not be proven, at least by human understanding for human comprehension . . . one must place geometry not with arithmetic, which stands purely *a priori,* but rather somewhat in the same rank with mechanics . . .[35]

Similarly, in a later remark, Gauss says:

> Exactly in the impossibility of deciding *a priori* between . . . Euclidean geometry . . . and S [Bolyai's absolute geometry] lies the clearest proof that Kant was wrong to maintain that space is only the form of our intuition.[36]

Lobachevsky, like Gauss, treats his new geometry as a theory that may be true of the space we live in[37] and is also aware that such a position is a serious challenge to apriorism. He says his geometrical theorems "can only be verified like all other physical laws by experiment, such as astronomical observations,"[38] and in fact he actually tries to assess measurements of certain stars to see if it can be decided which geometry is true.[39] Although the measurements seem to show that Euclidean geometry is true within the experimental error of his instruments, Lobachevsky is reluctant to rule out his new geometry. He even goes so far as to remark that we probably cannot know which geometry is true until we integrate the new geometry with a modified physics and test the whole thing. And then, he thinks, we may even find we need more than one geometry.[40]

At least Gauss and Lobachevsky, then, among the main workers in the "normal" mathematical tradition, raise important new questions for science and the philosophy of science on the basis of their discoveries. Physics is faced with the new problem of determining the true parallels postulate—either through direct measurement of figures in space (Gauss and Lobachevsky) or through the development and testing of new theories integrating Lobachevskian geometry into mechanics (Lobachevsky). Theories which had been developed by philosophers to explain the special "necessity" adhering to (Euclidean) geometrical propositions now seem clearly false, and so new explanations are needed of the special nature of mathematical truth and of the relation of mathematics to physics. What accounts for the difference between Reid and the geometers in their awareness of such related problems? I can offer only a speculative answer about what some of the factors may have been.

One obvious difference is that Reid begins with an interpretation or model, visible space, and develops a geometry for it, which turns out to be non-Euclidean. Starting with a model may be what leads Reid to think of his geometry as specifically tied to this particular model. In contrast, the mathematicians started with the negation of the parallels postulate and had the intention of showing that there is no model for what results, i.e., that it is inconsistent with the rest of the axioms.[41] When no contradictions appeared, and instead, an elaborate structure began to emerge from their work, they began to see analogies to certain other structures (for example, Johann Lambert's observations about the sphere and the imaginary sphere).[42] Nevertheless, no interpretations emerged until quite late, in the middle of the 19th century. We may speculate that psychologically this may have been a good thing, for it helped avoid the danger of Reid's procedure, in which some special (unintended) model assumes too great an importance. More importantly, since the parallels postulate itself had an intended interpretation according to which it was a statement about the space we live in, then starting with the negation of that postulate would not obviously lead one to think that the same physical interpretation is to be avoided. Rather, as counter-intuitive features of the emerging structure were discovered, such as the "absolute unit of length,"[43] the question seemed to come up immediately whether or not these features are realized in the space we live in. However much the original expectation was that there would be no interpretation of the new geometry, once a structure started to appear, it seemed obvious that the researchers should want to see whether or not our living space has that structure. After all, the geometrical sentences giving rise to it were sentences which normally purport to describe the world we live in.

Another source of difference may have a philosophical origin. Reid, as I show in Chapter V, has a nativist account of "first principles," such as the mathematical and logical principles central to geometry. He foreshadows Kant to a remarkable degree. Accordingly, it does *not* follow from his notion of first principles that if two equally consistent geometries appear, we must resort to experiment to decide which is true. Truths which derive from such first principles are not the sort of things we can hope to check by experiment. For Reid, both geometries are "true" since each is tied *a priori*, or "by our constitution," to a special interpretation, either tangible or visible space. In contrast, the mathematicians seemed to be in rebellion against the apriorism that had dominated German science after Kant. Gauss was obviously intimidated by it to some considerable extent, since he was afraid to publish. We cannot here attempt to explain why such a rebellion might have been taking place.

There is still one more point of contrast. Why was Reid's discovery of a non-Euclidean geometry itself neither fruitful nor important, either inside or outside his tradition? The context of its discovery appears to be the major factor in answering that question. The discovery is intimately tied to several related sets of problems, as I show in Chapters II-IV. Its main ideas are tied to 18th-century theory of mind, especially to Reid's attacks on the theory of concept formation central to the "ideal system." They are also tied to metaphysical arguments about idealism and realism surrounding the 18th-century theory of mind (see Chapter

IV). Its fine details are tied both to 18th-century theory of vision, especially the distance perception problem (Cf. Chapter II), and to 18th-century theory of mind, especially the theses about "heterogeneity" and "natural signs" (Cf. Chapter III). That is, both in its main ideas and in the details of its construction, it is presented as an auxiliary or corollary to special problems in Reid's tradition which have nothing to do with deciding what kind of space we live in. As I show in Chapter V, questions about the space we live in seemed to be further precluded by the nativistic or aprioristic philosophy of geometry Reid advances.

In contrast, the mathematicians were aware throughout their work that their problem was directly connected to the question, what are the geometrical properties of the space we live in? None of the problems in the theory of mind that confront Reid even raise the question whether or not common (Euclidean) geometry describes real (tangible) space. Visible space is not introduced by Reid as a competitor space to tangible space. It is two-dimensional, after all. And though visible space can be modeled on a subspace of tangible, Euclidean space (the surface of the sphere), Reid does not conceive of it as such a subspace. However "natural" the idea of extending a non-Euclidean geometry from two to three dimensions may seem to us, it was obviously not the "natural" thought for those who found the geometry introduced against the background of 18th-century theory of mind.

That such an extension of Reid's geometry was not naturally made, however, cannot count as evidence that Reid's discovery is not, after all, a discovery of a (two-dimensional) non-Euclidean geometry. That it was made in a different tradition as a result of solving different problems, and that it was not connected to the same set of new problems, does not make it any less the discovery of a non-Euclidean geometry.

Chapter II:

Reid & 18th Century Theory of Vision

1. *The Scientist of the Mind*

In Chapter I, I argue that Reid constructs a special visible space, develops a doubly elliptical geometry for this space, offers the surface of the sphere as a natural model for the geometry, and is fully aware that his geometry is a consistent alternative to Euclid's, even though he does not understand its significance. Although Reid was isolated from 18th-century work on the theory of parallels, his discovery does not just fall out of the sky. Rather, its roots lead us deep into the central problem of the *Inquiry*—Reid's effort to show that realism is compatible with the development of a true science of the human mind. In this chapter I take a close look at the kind of scientific practice Reid thinks is threatened by the idealism and skepticism of the Ideal System. In particular, I discuss in some detail the history of an important problem in 17th and 18th-century theory of vision, visual distance discrimination. Work on this problem provides Reid with the key technical features he needs for his construction in "The Geometry of Visibles."

The tradition in which Reid worked is a rather complex one. Problems in the psychology of perception, cognitive psychology, and epistemology are interwoven into comprehensive theories of the mind. The goal is to introduce the kind of order into our understanding of how the mind and the world interact that Newton had introduced into the study of the physical world.

Twentieth-century philosophers often have a biased view of these 17th and 18th-century theories. First, they see these theories only as they appear in the works of recognized philosophers like Descartes, Locke, Berkeley, Hume, and

Reid. Second, the effort is often made to isolate the timeless and "pure" philosophical problem from the historical dross of outdated psychological theory. In fact, however, the philosophers we single out were really participants in a more inclusive tradition; contributions to the construction of these vast theories of mind came from a variety of natural philosophers—physicists, anatomists, physiologists, and psychologists. Furthermore, the "pure" philosophical questions we are tempted to extract from their psychological settings were often integral components of the ongoing development of theory within the tradition and were often closely related to the actual practice of the researchers. For example, sometimes these philosophical questions led to the search for new mechanisms of concept formation or to the development of new learning theories. Sometimes philosophical beliefs held back that development. In other cases, the direction of influence went the other way: anatomical and psychological considerations affected, for example, the epistemological characterization of the "given" in visual perception, as I show in my discussion of the distance perception problem in the next section.

Some of the leading philosophers in the tradition, like Locke, Hume, and Reid, said themselves that their philosophical work was integrated into the broader practice of scientists. Locke thought that a scientific understanding of the capacities of the mind would let us move with greater surety in other sciences:

> were the capacities of our understandings well considered, the extent of our knowledge once discovered, and the horizon found which sets the bounds between the enlightened and dark parts of things; between what is and what is not comprehensible by us, men would perhaps with less scruple acquiesce in the avowed ignorance of the one, and employ their thoughts and discourse with more advantage and satisfaction in the other.[1]

Hume also claimed that the science of the human mind could provide a foundation for all other knowledge. He did not, however, believe that any special (philosophical) certainty adhered to the central truths developed in this science of the human mind. He accepted, for example, the missing shade of blue as a counter-example to one of his basic laws, which he could not have done if he thought these laws were logical truths or the results of logical analysis. Nor did Hume claim that there was any special (philosophical) method for attaining these central truths. Rather, the science of the human mind was able to provide the foundation for other sciences because it was thought to be a *central* science, not because the truths in it were thought to be certain or more certain than truths from other sciences or because the methods used in it were thought to provide any special guarantees. Both Berkeley and Hume, for example, sought to settle mathematical questions about the continuum by appeal to laws from the theory of mind. They also thought that a scientific moral philosophy would have to be founded on the knowledge gained about the formation of human beliefs, desires, and passions.

Consequently, the philosophers of this 17th and 18th-century tradition were not analysts of the "depth grammar" of our conceptual schemes; nor were they analysts of the logical structure of our theories. The philosophy that interested these men did not consist of some special set of "analytic" truths; nor did it consist of some special kind of *a priori* truths arrived at by special (philosophical) methods. Rather, the philosopher was the scientist of the mind.[2]

From the opening pages of the *Inquiry* it is clear that Reid views himself as just such a scientist of the mind. A substantial part of the argumentation in the *Inquiry* consists of observations on sensory phenomena, and a full third of the book, the bulk of the chapter on "seeing," is devoted to detailed discussion of the most up-to-date problems in 18th-century theory of vision. There are whole sections on "The parallel motion of the eyes," "seeing objects erect by inverted images," "seeing objects single with two eyes," "squinting," "single and double vision," visual distance discrimination, and the "laws of vision in brute animals."

Not only are these problems of considerable importance within the theory of vision, in that they are among the obvious phenomena that need explanation, but they also serve as important touchstones for testing, developing, and modifying the more comprehensive background theories of mind. For example, as I show in the next section, any purported explanation of distance perception committed the researcher to extensive assumptions about the kinds of operations the mind can perform. Consequently, in the course of explaining how distance perception works, researchers were forced to elaborate and modify important features of the background theory of mind, such as its learning theory and, of particular importance to the later development of epistemology, its notion of the "given" in perception.

As a scientist of the mind, Reid not only carries out research on these various problems, but he explicitly appeals to the dominant Newtonian methodology as a justification for his approach.

> Wise men now agree, or ought to agree in this, that there is but one way to the knowledge of nature's works; the way of observation and experiment . . . it is the only one by which any real discovery in philosophy can be made . . . |Newton's| *regulae philosophandi* are maxims of common sense, and are practiced every day in common life; and he who philosophizes by other rules, either concerning the material system, or concerning the mind, mistakes his aim.[3]

Reid takes his Newtonian strictures seriously and consistently warns against speculation on deep "causes." For example, he introduces his discussion of "seeing single with two eyes" with this remark:

> [I]n the solution of natural phenomena, all the length that the human faculties can carry us, is only this, that from particular phenomena, we may, by induction, trace out general phenomena, of which the particular ones are necessary consequences. And when we have arrived at the most general phenomena we can reach, there we must

stop . . . [These] laws of nature are nothing else but the
most general facts relating to the operations of nature
. . .[4]

Reid was not alone in his Newtonianism. The Scottish
schools of medicine of the period emphasized just such an
experimentalism as part of a more general program of
university reform imported from Holland. Large numbers of
Scottish medical students received their training in
Europe—especially in Dutch universities like Utrecht,
Franeker, Groningen and Leyden where men like Boerhaave
emphasized scientific experimentation and clinical instruction
in medicine.[5] The general methodological orthodoxy of the
day was based on Newton's "disavowal of hypothesis," and
Reid's university affiliations could hardly have left him
untouched by it.

This Newtonian, experimentalist tradition in which
Reid found himself seemed to him to be committed to some
version of realism. After all, without supposing that there is a
material world governed by objective laws and mechanisms,
what were these "particular" and "general" facts that were
being studied? The whole assumption behind the approach
was that God had actually created a material world and
designed the human mind, perhaps his most intricate
creation, so that it could interact with and learn about that
world. The point behind Newton's *regulae,* of sticking to
experimental phenomena and not engaging in speculation,
was to make sure we ended up understanding how God's
actual creations worked[6] and did not substitute
"speculation" for the search for real causes and mechanisms.
The very problems tackled by Reid—how we see single with
two eyes, how we make visual distance discriminations, how
we see objects upright instead of inverted, like the retinal
image—all presuppose the eye helps us to see a "real" world.
The problems seem to make little sense if all we ever really
"see" are our ideas, as Berkeley would have it.

Consequently, Reid wants no part of Berkeley's effort to
develop a phenomenalist reduction of science.[7] Berkeley

wanted to strip Newton's *regulae* of their realist rationale by claiming that the only "particular" phenomena we could study were sensations, and that the only "general facts" were regularities in the patterns of sensations. But Bishop Berkeley's attempt to "save" science by reconciling it to idealism was hardly the work of a saint. For it was Berkeley's sin—in fact the shared heresy of all proponents of the Ideal System—that had in the first place misled us, according to Reid, into thinking idealism was true. In subsequent chapters I show how Reid exposes this sin, the sin of accepting without proof a false theory of concept formation. But first I want to look in some detail at the history of the distance discrimination problem.

2. *The Distance Perception Problem*

In my analysis of the geometry of visibles I show that visible space is treated as a two-dimensional manifold. Reid insists that the eye can discriminate points having different "positions with regard to the eye." It cannot, however, discriminate points which have the same position with regard to the eye but are different distances from the eye. Reid thus introduces an equivalence relation, "same position with regard to the eye." We can construct two-dimensional visible space by "seeing" through The Eye used in Reid's construction and treating this equivalence relation as an identity relation, since we restrict ourselves to the discriminations The Eye can make.

The two-dimensionality of Reid's visible space has its basis in the claim that we do not, properly speaking, "see" the distance of objects, but rather that we judge the distance of the objects we see. This claim was a well-entrenched feature of late 17th-century theory of vision. Nevertheless, in the period between Descartes and Reid, there is a development and sharpening of the distinction between *seeing* and *judging* distance. The details of this development throw light on more than just the roots of Reid's discovery. Somewhat incidentally, but perhaps of more fundamental interest, the history also reveals how extensively the epistemological notion of the "given" in perception, influential even today, was a product of ongoing scientific work in 17th and 18th-century theory of vision. Conversely, we shall also see, in the debate between Berkeley and Reid, how philosophical biases about the "given" affect the development of the scientific work.

In Descartes' explanation[8] (1637) of visual distance discrimination there is some slurring over of the difference between *seeing* and *judging*. Descartes says there are four "means" by which we make visual distance discriminations. Two of them—information on the shape of the eye transmitted to the brain by nerve impulses, and information on the clarity and distinctness of the object—seem to require elaborate learning processes of two distinct sorts. Information on eye shape is presumably something of which we are not conscious on Descartes' view, and so we need a learning theory that can handle this type of non-conscious information. Information on the clarity and distinctness of the object is something we are conscious of (sensations), and so we need a learning theory that can handle conscious inputs. Not only does Descartes not distinguish these "means" according to the type of input, conscious or non-conscious, but he also does not even note the need for describing these learning processes, leaving a significant gap in his theory. As I show below, awareness of the need for describing these processes grows after Descartes.

Descartes' third "means" by which we make distance discriminations is information about the position of the eyes (angle of convergence), presumably also relayed to the brain. It is not clear whether or not we are supposed to be conscious of this input. Nevertheless, knowledge of this angle enters into a (subconscious) calculation by "natural geometry," a calculation contained "implicitly" in a "simple act of imagination."[9] Some later theorists argued that convergence was important, but they rejected the elaborate and implausible mental acts and operations that would have to accompany the use of geometry in some subconscious way.

Later theorists wanted to pack fewer such innate abilities into the mental machine. Instead they stressed the fact that convergence would be accompanied by "impressions" or "sensations" of eye position. The presence of such sensations meant that the role of convergence could be explained by the same kind of learning theory that handled all conscious inputs.

Two of the three Cartesian "means" of distance discrimination discussed so far—eye shape and convergence information—involve information which cannot be traced back to the (retinal) image formed in the eye. Although he is not very clear on the point, Descartes seems to recognize that retinal information is itself not sufficient to permit distance discrimination. In contrast to later theorists, however, Descartes speaks of the processes involved in all these means, including what I have called the "information processing" of non-retinal information, as "*seeing* distance" by the various "means." "*Seeing* distance" is contrasted with "imagining (judging) distance" only in the case of the fourth "means," knowledge of the size or position of the object gained from another source. Thus, for Descartes, *seeing* may well involve a variety of deeper information processes, and the contrast with *imagining* or *judging* is not based on the distinction between the presence or absence of deeper (non-retinal) information processes. Consequently, Descartes' version of what we, strictly speaking, *see*, that is, what is *given* in vision alone, will not be the same notion as that which is based on the distinction between retinal and non-retinal information processing.

Many later theorists did restrict the use of "seeing." "Seeing," properly understood, gives us only that information which the late 17th and 18th-century researcher can claim is contained in, or originates in, the retinal image or impression. Thus, in accordance with certain crude anatomical considerations, these theorists draw a line between kinds of information processing—retinal as opposed to deeper processing—and thus lay the basis for sharpening the distinction between that which is *given* in experience and that which is based on deeper, coordinating and learning processes. Complementary to the sharpening of the notion of the *given* was the more careful attention paid to the nature of the deeper processes. Among these deeper processes lay the explanations of how we coordinate information from different sensory inputs—say, tactual and kinesthetic with visual. Much of the empiricist learning theory and theory of concept formation would have to be concerned with these processes. But we are getting a bit ahead of our history of distance perception.

Malebranche was one of the chief contributors to the tradition of problem solving activities we are considering.[10] We are interested in three features of Malebranche's discussion of distance discrimination. First, Malebranche shows some recognition of the gap I have pointed out in Descartes' theory. That is, Malebranche attempted to give some description of the processes involved in making use of the "means" of distance discrimination. Second, Malebranche attempted to explain why we make so many mistakes in certain kinds of distance discriminations. In so doing, he provides a diagram systematizing these cases of failure that is strikingly suggestive of Reid's construction. But third, the differences between Malebranche's and Reid's uses of a similar construction illustrate the progress that was to be made in the intervening one hundred years in sharpening the distinction between the visual given and deeper information processing. This last point gives us a way of describing just what Reid's visual space is from the point of view of 18th-century theory of vision: it is a model of what is given in visual perception.

Malebranche seems to recognize the gap in Descartes' theory when he proposes a new mental act or operation, the "natural judgment," which is supposed to explain how we make use of the "Media" of distance discrimination, like Descartes' first three "means." In fact, Malebranche's "natural judgments" are really much like Descartes' subconscious calculations by a natural geometry, although they are extended to include utilization of the other "means" as well. In addition to extending these operations to include other, analogous processes, Malebranche attempts to describe what the "natural judgment" consists of. He says that these "natural judgments" are "sensations," but they are sensations of a special sort, namely they are "compounded sensations."[11] By explaining that we are here concerned with *compounded* sensations, Malebranche indicates that there is something, the processes involved in such compounding, which must really be studied here. But the only thing Malebranche tells us about these processes is that they take place at a level which does not directly interact with "Reason." As Malebranche puts it, "Natural judgments of sight," such as the judgment that the moon seems to be very little when directly overhead, are "built upon perceptions of the same sight, and Reason cannot correct them."[12]

Postulation of such natural judgments hardly explains what these processes are, appealing as it does to an unsatisfying model of an internal judge. Still, it is a crude recognition of the gap left in Descartes' account. Its importance is that it shows more clearly that there is a new problem area for the researcher in the tradition—the proper analysis of these deeper processes.

Malebranche's discussion of distance discrimination falls into three parts.[13] First he modifies Descartes' list of four "means" of judging distance and arrives at a new list of six "Media". The details of these modifications are not important here. Next, Malebranche offers a diagram which divides into cases the kinds of errors we make in attempting visual distance discriminations. Finally, Malebranche argues that he can account for each case of error by explaining how one of the relevant "Media" is not of use in that case. In effect, this is an attempt to prove that the list of six "Media" is complete and explains adequately our distance discrimination abilities.

The diagram Malebranche provides is strikingly suggestive of Reid's construction, in which he places an eye at the center of a hollow sphere. Since Reid often refers to Malebranche, it is very likely he actually saw Malebranche's diagram.[14] We might speculate that this discussion of distance discrimination errors in Malebranche may have provided Reid with the basic idea for his actual construction. Malebranche's diagram and his discussion of it are worth reproducing at length here as evidence for that speculation:

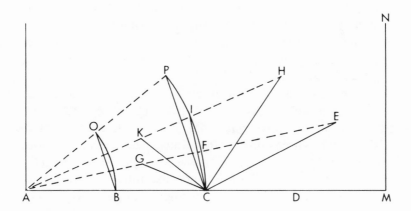

Let A be the eye of the beholder, C the object which I suppose at a considerable distance from A. I say that though the Object remains immovable in C, he may believe it as distant as D, or as near as B; and though the object should recede to D, or approach to B, he might believe it immovable in C; . . . And although the object advances from C, to E,H,G, or K, he may believe that it is only mov'd from C to F, or I . . . But if the object be moved in a line equally distant from the beholder, that is by a circumference, whose center should be the eye of the beholder, although the object move from C to P, he may believe that it moves only from B to O; and on the contrary, if it moves from B to O, he may believe it moves from C to P.[15]

The parallel between Malebranche's diagram and description and Reid's construction is obvious.

Although Reid and Malebranche appeal to rather similar models, they do so with important differences. These differences in treatment reflect a difference in the degree to which the notion of the *given* in vision has been sharpened in the intervening one hundred years. Malebranche argues that we sometimes, or often, may not be able to make the required discriminations. In contrast, Reid claims that the eye, "vision alone," can make *no* such discriminations at all. Malebrache's problem is to explain the mistakes we do make by reference to the ways in which the "Media" which affect our "natural judgments" are often misleading. That is, he wants to show that, although the "Media" help us in some cases, we can see just why they break down in these other cases. Reid, on the other hand, is using his construction to illustrate in a precise way what is available to us in "pure vision." His whole construction illustrates an accepted point of theory: that the given in vision, properly restricted, provides no basis at all for distance discrimination. In fact, we could say that the geometry of visibles is the geometry of what is *given* in vision. Reid would agree with some of Malebranche's analysis of the "Media" of distance judgment, improving on it by appeal to developments within the tradition. Still, discussion of these "Media" of discrimination had become, by Reid's time, sharply distinguished from the analysis of what is given in "visual sensation." In sum, Malebranche's diagram presents a suggestive starting point for Reid's construction, even if the theoretical developments of a century gave Reid a different perspective on the diagram from that of Malebranche.

We noted that Malebranche differed from Reid in that he did not possess as sharply a defined notion of the visual given as Reid. Some thirty years after Malebranche, Dr. William Molyneux gave a clear statement to that sharpened notion of the *given*. He said,

> Distance of itself, is not to be perceived; for 'tis a line (or a length) presented to our eye with its end toward us, which must therefore be only a *point*, and that is invisible.[16]

By the time Molyneux's clarification reaches Reid, it no longer leads to the conclusion that distance is a point and is therefore "invisible." Rather, it is converted into the observation that all real points on a ray to the center of the eye can affect only one point on the retina, giving "the eye" no basis for distinguishing them. The effect is the same: we do not see points at different distances from the eye, and so we do not "see distance."

Literature on the distance perception problem has, by the 1690's, already provided two main sources for Reid's construction. Malebranche's diagram contains the main ideas behind Reid's introduction of the equivalence relation, "same position with regard to the eye," and thus the technical basis for treating visual space as two-dimensional. Molyneux's remarks sharpen the notion of the given in vision, which is the development clear in Reid but still missing in Malebranche.

In the rest of my history I discuss briefly certain later developments which further clarify the notion of the given and show more sophistication in handling the deeper information processes. It was this ongoing work whose credibility Reid wanted to save from the threat of idealism and skepticism. But I also show that even *within* the theory of vision there was an attack on the effects of Berkeley's idealism.

We can begin by noting some small advances made by Molyneux in describing the kinds of processes involved in making distance discriminations. Molyneux divides the distance perception problem into two parts—distance discrimination of near and of distant objects. He argues that if an object is so far away that the "interval between our two eyes, bears no sensible proportion" to the distance of the object, or if we are using monocular vision, then "the estimate we make of the distance of objects . . . is rather the act of our judgment than our senses."[17] We acquire this ability to estimate by an "act of judgment" through "exercises and a faculty of comparing." It is not a "natural" ability. Subsumed under this category of discriminations are those which rely on several of the "means" or "Media" Descartes and Malebranche had listed: interjacent bodies, estimates of

comparative magnitude, faintness of colors. The advantage of
this grouping is that it seems to collect those "means" which
can all be handled by a similar learning process.

There remains the category of near distance
discriminations, those in which the distance of the objects
bears a "sensible proportion" to the "interval of the eyes."
Here Molyneux is somewhat unclear, saying only that the
distance of the near objects is "perceived by the turn of the
eyes, or by the angle of the optick axes."[18] Since Molyneux has
already said that we do not *see* distance at all, distinguishing
his treatment sharply from Descartes', he must here be
concerned with an ability to *judge*. Further, since he has also
contrasted these cases with those involving "*acquired* abilities,"
he must here mean that our "perception" of differences in
near distances is based on a set of "*natural*" abilities. It is not
clear whether or not Molyneux considers these "natural"
processes or abilities to be fixed from birth or to be capable of
developing through practice. At any rate, Molyneux would
seem to contrast the non-conscious information input in these
cases with the obviously conscious inputs for far distance
discrimination. Since he says nothing on this point, we should
assume that he agrees with Descartes that the inputs from
convergence are not conscious. At any rate, Molyneux does
seem to contrast the near distance discriminations, which are
"acts of sense," with far distance discriminations, which are
"acts of judgment." This distinction supports the claim that
the processes involved are of a very different sort from those
connected with far distance discriminations. On this interpretation, it is still clear that some complicated, un-
analysed processes go on which make up the "act of sense."
These processes are not described, although they presumably
go on at a sub- or pre-conscious level, and are therefore
distinguishable from acts of judgment.

Berkeley, in his discussion of distance perception in *New
Theory of Vision*, attempts to introduce a major simplification
of the theory of distance perception. Prior to Berkeley, all
researchers had listed "means" or "Media" which can be

divided into two sorts: one kind involves information inputs of which we are conscious, the other sort involves inputs of which we are not conscious. Different types of learning theories, requiring respectively different types of mental mechanisms, are needed to account for these two types of inputs. Berkeley, however, insists that the only kind of inputs than can have an effect on us are ones of which we are conscious (or can become conscious of if we pay attention correctly). As Berkeley puts it, "it is *evident* that no idea which is not itself perceived can be the means of perceiving any other idea."[19]

Using this "evident" principle, so important to his basic idealist position, Berkeley argues that the accounts offered by his predecessors all depend at some point on inputs of which we are not conscious, which are not themselves "perceived." For example, Berkeley explicitly attacks the claim that perception of the degree of convergence or divergence of impinging rays enters into any "calculation" of the distance of an object. Similarly, we do not "perceive" the angle of convergence of our optic axes. In each of these cases, however, we do have sets of sensations—sensations of the distinctness or confusedness of the visual object or sensations of tension in eye muscles—which are associated "by custom" with different distances. Such sensations are not "necessarily" related to particular distances: there is no *a priori* calculation by means of which we could compute a given distance for a given sensation as input. Rather, we associate sensations with distances through experience. Accordingly, we need a learning theory that can account for our ability to coordinate "confused" and "distinct" visual sensations with distance information received through our tactual senses.

Berkeley's attempted simplification of the theory, in which he tries to show that there is only one kind of deep process involved, is compatible with his accepting Molyneux's claim that the eye itself does not receive sufficient information to permit distance discriminations. There is a difference, however, between Berkeley's and Reid's account of what follows from the fact that the eye itself,[20] without the aid of experience, cannot make distance discriminations. Berkeley claims that the visual objects given in purely visual perception are "in the mind." The "primary" objects of sight "neither are, nor appear to be, without the mind or at any distance off."[21] His argument is that, since we can make no visual distance discriminations without appeal to information from other sources, then we cannot have any "idea" of objects at a distance from us that is not derived from the *other* senses. Berkeley backs up this claim with a special argument which we shall look at in more detail in Chapters III and IV, namely the argument that since color is "in the mind," and (our ideas of) color and extension are inseparable, then extension is also "in the mind."

Reid, however, does not agree with Berkeley's conclusion. He does agree that the eye itself, without the aid of experience, cannot make distance discriminations. From this Reid concludes, as I show, that the eye itself (The Eye of the construction, for example) sees all visible points as if they were equidistant.[22] It does not see points, however, as if they are no distance at all from the eye, that is, "in the mind" as Berkeley would have it. Rather Reid claims that "by our constitution" we assume visible objects are "outside" of us: we have an innate propensity, given certain experiences, to perceive visual objects as external to us. On this point of disagreement with Berkeley, Reid seems to draw on the work of W. D. Porterfield, a physician whose *Treatise on the Eye* is the acknowledged mid-18th-century classic on the subject. Porterfield argues,

> In feeling objects, the Mind, by means of an original and conate law, to which it has always been subjected, traces back to its own perceptions, not only from the sensorium to the retina, but from thence also outwards towards the object itself, along right lines drawn perpendicularly to the retina from every point of it on which any impression is made by the rays forming the picture; by which means the mind or visible faculty does always see every point of the object, not in the sensorium or retina, but without the eye, in these perpendicular lines.[23]

I return to Porterfield's and Reid's nativism and the sense in which they anticipate Kant in Chapter V. All that is important here is Reid's disagreement with Berkeley on this question of what is *given* in experience.

Reid's own discussion of distance perception is our strongest evidence that extensive problem-solving activity continued to be focused on the question during the 18th century. Reid mentions three main works concerned with distance perception following Berkeley, which shows that he was thoroughly familiar both with the history of the problem and the live questions that still made the problem an appealing one. First, Reid refers to the anatomical work of Dr. James Jurin, who described the role of muscle contractions in focusing the eye.[24] The details of this work do not concern us, for the only point Reid draws on is that these muscle motions must be sensible and thus provide a set of "signs" by means of which we can make certain distance discriminations. A second major work Reid often cites is Robert Smith's *Compleat System of Opticks*.[45] Reid claims it is an improvement over Berkeley's account, especially on the role of visible or apparent magnitude in determining distance discriminations.[26] But the third major work, Porterfield's *Treatise on the Eye*[27] is clearly the most important sustained effort to explain the nature of the deeper processes of information processing, and we shall discuss briefly his main contributions.

Berkeley had simply appealed to "custom" as a mechanism by which certain sensations became "signs" for certain distances. Porterfield, a physician, was interested in explaining in greater detail what was meant by "custom." He discusses, for example, the role of eye muscle contractions in focusing the eye. Porterfield argues that by repeated trials, the mind "finds out the precise place [the crystalline] ought to possess for rendering our sight as distinct as possible."[28] In other words, these motions of the crystalline are *voluntary*. The question arises, however, how can we have voluntary control over "motions" of which we are not conscious? Porterfield answers that "there are many other motions that are no doubt voluntary and depending on our Mind, of which

we are every bit as little conscious."[29] He gives as other
examples the motions of the eye lid and the muscle
contractions which "tune the ear." Thus Porterfield really
gives no evidence to back up his answer but rather shows that
he is taking it to be a well-established law that all "motions"
are voluntarily controlled by the mind.[30] Porterfield's account
relies, then, on the development of a skill through repeated
practice of motions which are voluntarily controlled. His
account of custom assimilates these mechanisms in vision to
all other acquired skills. Because these motions are so
extensively practiced, they "come at last always to accompany
one another, and that so necessarily as to make it impossible
for us to separate them by any act of volition."[31] At other
points, Porterfield does not say that it becomes "impossible,"
but only that it appears so: "such is the power of custom and
habit, that many actions which are no doubt voluntary, and
proceed from our Mind, are in certain circumstances rendered
so necessary as to appear altogether mechanical and
independent of our wills."[32]

Two related question arise with regard to Porterfield's
account. First, if "volitions" are operative here, should we not
be conscious of them? Second, in some cases the associated
"signs" or inputs are not things of which we are conscious, so
how does Porterfield meet Berkeley's objection that we must
be conscious of all such inputs or "signs"?

Porterfield is sensitive to these questions but appears to
hedge in his answers to them. On the one hand he says we are
not "in a common way of speaking"[33] *conscious* of these
inputs or volitions. This answer suggests there is some other
sense of "conscious" that does apply, but Porterfield is
reluctant to explain what that might be:

> But without determining how far the thoughts and
> operations of the mind may or may not imply
> consciousness, which is a metaphysical question I leave
> to be disputed . . . it is sufficient for my present purpose,
> to have shown in a few of many instances that might have
> been brought, are motions unquestionably voluntary and

depending on the mind, which by custom and habit have become so easy as to be performed without our knowledge or attention.[34]

On the other hand, Porterfield sometimes says there is no consciousness at all:

There are many motions that unquestionably depend on the volitions of the mind, and yet these volitions are not attended with any remarkable consciousness; the want of such consciousness is, therefore, no good argument against the mind's being the cause of the motions of the pupil for example .[35]

Earlier, we saw that anatomical considerations influenced the epistemological notion of the given in vision. Now, there is the opposite influence: in Porterfield's discussion of sensations of which we have no "remarkable" consciousness, we see philosophical prejudices affect the development of the theory of mind. The idealism of the period, sharpened by Berkeley, required that all inputs to the mind be conscious. The idealism thus seems to have forced researchers to ignore the obvious fact that we are not conscious of many inputs that nevertheless do contribute to our knowledge and to the exercise of our abilities. Porterfield was waging an uphill fight against that idealism and more or less gave in to it. Reid's "material impression," of which we are definitely not conscious but which "suggests" certain concepts to us, is a bolder step against the idealists' effort to say that all sensory inputs must be conscious. Berkeley's idealist simplification was no help to the development of 18th-century science of the mind.

Although Porterfield's discussion of these points concerns topics other than the one that mainly concerns us—distance perception—the conclusions he comes to transfer directly to his discussion of distance perception, since some of the "means" involve inputs to which we do not normally attend in any "remarkable" way. Further, his discussion of custom also applies to distance discrimination.

Instead of repeating these points in their application to
Porterfield's account of distance perception, I turn now to
Reid's discussion and show how it has been influenced by
Porterfield's.

Reid accepts the second of Porterfield's answers to the
question, how conscious are we of the motions of the eye
responsible for producing distant vision?

> These motions were at first voluntary and unconfined;
> but as the intention of nature was, to produce perfect and
> distinct vision by their means, we soon learn by
> experience to regulate them according to that
> intention only, without the least reflection.[36]

Even if we are not conscious of these motions that adjust the
eye, we are, Reid argues,

> conscious of the effort employed in producing these
> motions; and probably have some sensation which
> accompanies them, to which we give as little attention as
> to other sensations. And thus, an effort consciously
> excited, or a sensation consequent upon that effort,
> comes to be conjoined with the distance of the object
> which gave occasion to it, and by this conjuction
> becomes a sign of that distance.[37]

Of course, the "distance" that is "conjoined" with the
sensation (that accompanies focus and accommodation) is a
distance established by *other* modalities than vision. Reid is
here clearly following Berkeley's and Porterfield's accounts,
but he is also aware of a further question that might arise.
Berkeley had been careful to distinguish *judging* distance from
seeing distance. Does Porterfield's account of custom,
however, make it inappropriate to talk about judgments? As
Reid puts it, "we are at a loss whether to call them by the name
of *judgment,* or by that of *simple perception.*"[38]

Reid responds by claiming,

> It is not worthwhile to dispute about names; but it is
> evident that my belief, both first and last, was produced

rather by signs than by arguments; and that the mind
proceeded to the conclusion in both cases by habit, and
not by ratiocination.[39]

The importance of the distinction between seeing and judging
was, as we have seen, based on the distinction between
information all of which could be traced to the retinal
image and information not all of which could be so traced,
and instead included other inputs. In cases of distance
discrimination, it is clear that we require non-retinal inputs,
and so we have a case of judging. The question is whether
"judging" is a good term for processes which are not entirely
conscious. Reid passes this question off as a quibble, but it is
clear both from his awareness of the question and his answer
to it that he is thoroughly familiar with the issues surrounding
the whole question of distance perception.

In this discussion of the 150-year history of the visual
distance discrimination problem several important points
emerge. First, the sources for two central features of Reid's
construction of visible space can be found in the literature on
distance perception. In particular, Malebranche's diagram of
the different cases of distance discrimination failures is highly
suggestive of Reid's whole construction. The point missing
from Malebranche's account, that there is no basis in retinal
information for distance discriminations, is supplied by
Molyneux. Thus, Reid's visible space can be interpreted as a
model of what is given in vision, and the geometry of visibles,
accordingly, describes the mathematical properties of the
visual given. Second, the history of the distance perception
problem shows how a notion of some importance to
epistemology, the notion of the given in vision, develops and is
sharpened as a result of developments in the theory of vision
deriving from anatomy and physiology. Complementary to
that development is the elaboration of those deeper
information processing operations to be distinguished from
the surface processes of "pure vision." But here the
development is in turn influenced by Berkeley's idealism.
Berkeley's attempt to reduce all such processes to operations

on conscious inputs, and Porterfield's basic support of that account, were major 18th-century developments influencing Reid's account of distance perception.

Since Reid's construction draws, as we have seen, on features within this problem solving tradition, we can begin to see that his mathematical discovery *is* related to "relevant" scientific practice, even if not to work on the theory of parallels. In subsequent chapters I further link Reid's discovery to the practice within his tradition.

My detailed discussion of the distance perception problem provides further evidence of the point with which I begin this chapter: Reid views himself as a scientist of the mind, one who can make little sense of his work without a realist stance. The distance perception problem is a prime example of the kind of scientific practice Reid felt to be fundamentally threatened by idealism.

Chapter III:

Reid's Response to Berkeley

1. *Reid and Berkeley on the Object of Geometry*

I have shown in Chapter II some of the ways in which Reid's construction in "The Geometry of Visibles" draws for its technical details on 18th-century theory of vision. But with the exception of some brief remarks in Chapter I, Sec. 2, it is not yet clear why Reid is motivated to develop his geometry at all nor why he thinks that developing the geometry will strengthen his case for realism in the *Inquiry*. In the next two chapters I investigate in detail two ways in which Reid thinks the geometry of visibles can be used as a weapon against idealism. First, Reid is intent on answering the arguments for idealism regarding visual space Berkeley put forward in his *Essay Toward a New Theory of Vision*. In this chapter, I show that Reid's exposition in "The Geometry of Visibles" is a point by point refutation of some of Berkeley's arguments in that early work. In Chapter IV, I show how Reid uses his geometry to attack the very underpinnings of Berkeleyan and Humean idealism and skepticism—their theory of concept formation. That is, Reid has a very important reason for making the point that the visibles can be studied mathematically.

2. *The Background to the Argument*

In Sect. 149 of the *New Theory of Vision*, Berkeley poses the following question:

> We have shown there is no such idea as that of extension in abstract, and that there are two kinds of sensible extension and figures which are entirely distinct and heterogeneous from each other. Now it is natural to inquire which of these is the object of geometry.[1]

47

Berkeley goes on to argue that, although some considerations might lead us to think geometry has as its object visible figure and extension, in fact the object of geometry is tangible figure and extension. Indeed, he tries to show there cannot be a geometry of visible figure and extension. Before I look at his arguments for these conclusions (see next section) I show why Berkeley wanted the answer he gives, why Reid wanted to answer the question and provide a different answer, and why the question about the object of geometry might remain of interest independently of Berkeley's own particular ontological claims in the *New Theory of Vision*.

First, it will help to restate Berkeley's question. Assume that a wire triangle is situated in a plane perpendicular to one's line of sight and occupies the central portion of the visual field. The immediate object of sight, for Berkeley, is the given colored expanse whose figure in this case is triangular. In Sect. 43 of *New Theory of Vision,* Berkeley argues that it is impossible for us even "in thought, to separate and abstract color from extension." But then, since "it seems agreed on all hands" that color is "not without the mind," we are forced, according to Berkeley, to conclude that visible figure and extension will also be "in the mind."[2] That is, we can take the immediate object of sight, the triangular colored expanse, to be a sense-datum.[3] On the other hand, we may also touch the wire triangle and have the tactual experience of a triangular object. In the *New Theory of Vision,* however, unlike in Berkeley's later *Principles,* the tangible extension and figure are left "outside the mind," as properties of objects taken to be "external" to the mind. On this interpretation, the *New Theory of Vision* can be described as a halfway house to immaterialism or idealism[4]: objects of vision are "in" but objects of touch are "out." Berkeley's question, then, is this: which sensible figure, the visible one "in the mind" or the tangible one "outside the mind," is the kind of figure whose properties are demonstrated in the science of geometry.

Given Berkeley's goal in the *New Theory of Vision* of establishing idealism with regard to objects of vision, but maintaining realism (materialism) with regard to objects of touch, it is not difficult to see why he would want to show that tangible, not visible, figure and extension is the "object of geometry." It is the world of tangible objects, the external, "material" world, which we must come to understand if we are to "regulate our actions in order to attain those things necessary to the preservation and well-being of our bodies, as also to avoid whatever may be hurtful and destructive of them."[5] Our common sense knowledge of this material world is systematized and extended through scientific experiment and observation. Both our practical and theoretical sciences involve geometry, however. But then it would seem obvious that geometry, since it is applied in these sciences, describes the properties of tangible objects. To be sure, objects of vision are of great aid in extending our knowledge of tangible objects: according to Berkeley, objects of vision act as "natural signs" for objects of touch, signs which we learn to associate with tangible objects as soon as we enter life.

It might be thought that these natural signs, the objects of vision, could be the objects of geometry. But this alternative is not acceptable to Berkeley in *New Theory of Vision*. It would force him into a skepticism with regard to the mathematical properties of tangible objects that he wants to avoid at all costs at this point in the presentation of his theories. The skeptical argument derives from the claim that there are no "necessary connections" between objects of vision and objects of touch, that is, between the "natural signs" and the things signified. In particular, visible and tangible figures could not both have the properties described by geometry since that would amount to the existence of a "necessary connection" in the form of shared, demonstrable properties. If we assume it is the "signs" (visible figures) that are the objects of geometry, then the things signified (tangible figures) cannot be the object of geometry and cannot have the mathematical properties geometry demonstrates. Consequently, we should be left knowing nothing of the geometrical properties of material bodies on this assumption. To avoid such a skeptical conclusion, which would cast doubt on the halfway house ontology of *New Theory of Vision,* Berkeley argues that geometry has tangible figures, the "things signified", as its object and, consequently, that visible figures cannot be the object of geometry.

For Berkeley, then, proving that visible figure and extension could not be mathematical objects would serve as an indirect corroboration of his claim that objects of vision are "in the mind" not "in the external world." Reid's main purpose in the *Inquiry*, however, is to show that a form of realism is compatible with a scientific approach to the study of the human mind. The main thrust of argumentation in the *Inquiry* is intended to show that Berkeley, Hume, and other proponents of the Ideal System, as he referred to their theory of mind, are led to idealism and skepticism by a false theory of concept formation, one which places undue emphasis on the role of sensations. As part of his general defense of realism, Reid wants to show, contra Berkeley in *New Theory of Vision*, that there is no ontological dichotomy between objects of vision and objects of touch. Reid wants to show that both kinds of objects are "real" and "external" to the mind. On Reid's view, it seems natural to ask why we should not be able to study visibles mathematically, much as we can study tangibles. Showing that there is indeed a geometry of visibles would counter Berkeley's suggestion that the impossibility of such a geometry counts as indirect evidence for visible figure and extension being "in the mind."

The weakness of Reid's case is that it appears to be strictly *ad hominem.* At best, showing that tangibles and visibles can equally well be studied mathematically can count as an argument for realism only if there is an independent argument establishing realism for all geometrical objects. In fact, neither Berkeley, in *New Theory of Vision,* nor Reid, in the *Inquiry*, offers any such argument. Consequently, Reid's construction of the geometry of visibles, as an answer to Berkeley's question, is really a defensive move: far from establishing an independent argument *for* realism, it merely shows that Berkeley's argument about the "object of geometry" cannot, taken by itself, count as evidence *against* realism with regard to visible space. At best, Reid's argument can be viewed as an effort to shift back to Berkeley the burden of proving that visibles are "in the mind."

As I show, Berkeley introduces his question about the object of geometry as a corollary to his demonstration of the distinctness and heterogeneity of tangible and visible figures and extension. Given the ontology of the *New Theory of Vision*, it is natural to construe the "heterogeneity" thesis to mean that visible objects and tangible objects are representatives of two distinct genera: mental objects and material objects, respectively. And I show why, on this interpretation, Berkeley and Reid both give the answers they do to the question about the "object of geometry." But Berkeley continues to support the heterogeneity thesis and the accompanying doctrine of natural signs even after the half-way house idealism of *New Theory of Vision* (visibles "in" and tangibles "out") is dropped in *The Principles* (visibles and tangibles both "in"). And Reid talks of heterogeneity and natural signs from a realist perspective (visibles and tangibles both "out"). So I owe an explanation of why the heterogeneity thesis, to which the question about the "object of geometry" is "corollary," should live on and be of interest to either Berkeley or Reid once it is stripped of its ontological bite.

The "heterogeneity" thesis, stripped of its ontological implications, continues to be of interest to Berkeley and Reid because it indicates an important problem in 18th-century theory of concept formation.[6] Let us construe the "heterogeneity" thesis to mean that a different genus of objects is determined by each sense modality. This reading is acceptable to Berkeley in the *Principles*, for whom objects of touch and vision are distinct genera of sense data, and to Reid, for whom visible and tangible figures are distinct genera of "external" objects. Viewed in this way, the thesis of heterogeneity calls attention to a perplexing problem faced by the 18th-century cognitive-psychologist—epistemologist in Berkeley and Reid's tradition: how do we "derive" our "idea(s)" of space or extension from completely different ("heterogeneous") sets of sensory inputs, tactual and visual?

If only one genus of input is relevant to the genesis of an "idea" like that of space or extension, then it might be at least plausible to speak of ideas as "copies" of sensations. But how can such ideas be copies of sensory inputs from distinct genera? This type of problem forces the researcher to worry about mental processes of a different type from those that might work within each sense modality. Eventually the researcher must develop a sophisticated learning theory that can account for the ways in which heterogeneous sensory inputs are coordinated. The 18th-century philosopher could, then, cling to the thesis of "heterogeneity" without the ontological interpretation of *New Theory of Vision*, as signalling a serious problem in learning theory.

The Berkeleyan doctrine that immediate objects of vision serve as "natural signs" for tangible objects may be viewed as an attempt to skirt this problem of finding mechanisms that can coordinate "heterogeneous" inputs. On this view, visible figure and tangible figure are "naturally" coordinated as "sign" to "thing signified." Perhaps we cannot help but feel that little is explained by this doctrine. Still, Reid did cling to the "heterogeneity" thesis and to the accompanying doctrine of natural signs.

Since Berkeley had first raised the question about the object of geometry as a "corollary" to these theses, and since Reid retains an interest in them, it is not surprising that the geometry of visibles is introduced by Reid as a confirmation of certain general features of these theses and as a clarification of certain specific points concerning them. When Reid shows that two different geometries are needed to describe tangible and visible figures, he claims he has made precise the sense in which the two genera of objects are distinct: the mathematical properties of the one are not the mathematical properties of the other.[7] On the other hand, for relatively small figures, it is difficult to detect sensible differences between the visible and tangible figures. Consequently a rough "similitude" holds between the "natural signs" and the "things signi-fied"—contrary to Berkeley's claim that there is no simil-itude between visible and tangible objects.[8] These rather minor results are all that Reid notes as the immediate payoff from the discovery of the (non-Euclidean) geometry of visibles, developed as it was to answer Berkeley's "corollary" question. The importance of the geometry was never taken to exceed the importance of the theses of heterogeneity and natural signs to which it was "corollary."

With these motivational remarks out of the way, we can turn to Berkeley's actual arguments concerning the 'object of geometry' and to Reid's replies.

3. *Berkeley's Argument*

Berkeley argues in two stages that visible figures are not the objects of geometry. In the first stage of his argument, in section 151 of the *New Theory of Vision*, Berkeley cites three points for which he had argued earlier in sections 59, 60, and 61:

(a) "visible extensions in themselves are little regarded."

(b) visible extensions "have no settled determinate greatness."

(c) "men measure altogether by the application of tangible extension."

There are two distinct positions Berkeley might want to establish. First, he might want to argue that although visible figure and extension could be objects of geometrical study, in fact we usually do not pay any attention to them. Let us call the claim that visible figure and extension are not the usual objects of geometry, though one could make them objects of geometrical demonstrations, the Weak Negative Thesis. In contrast, there is a Strong Negative Thesis that visible figure and extension are not the kinds of things which can be objects of geometrical study. Now if the Weak Negative Thesis were true, and if one never thought that there might be geometries other than common (Euclidean) geometry, then one would be forced to assume that visible and tangible figures and extension would have to share certain mathematical ("necessary") properties, contrary to the thesis of distinctness and heterogeneity. So we might expect Berkeley to argue for the Strong Negative Thesis.

A glance at Berkeley's points (a)-(c), however, shows that he does not seem to be arguing for the Strong Negative Thesis. Point (a), that visible extensions are little regarded, seems irrelevant to the Strong Negative Thesis, although it is obviously compatible with the Weak Negative Thesis. Indeed, Reid accepts (a) in his presentation of the geometry of visibles and uses it to explain why no one had previously noticed that the visibles have a geometry, in fact a non-Euclidean geometry.[9] In other words, Reid uses (a) to explain why no one had seen the Weak Negative Thesis was true.

Berkeley's argument for point (b), that visible extensions "have no settled determinate greatness," also falls short of being an argument for the Strong Negative Thesis. To establish (b), Berkeley argues that a given visible extension, which we may take to be an arc containing a given number of degrees of the visual field, can be associated with tangible objects of different sizes. For example, place objects one inch long and one foot long at appropriate distances from the eye and both can be made to occupy identical portions of the visual field. It should be obvious that Berkeley's argument does not prove that visible extensions or figures do not have determinate magnitudes. In fact, Berkeley's argument implies just the opposite. We do have a way of judging that the visible extensions are equivalent or we would not be able to associate the different tangible extensions with the *same* visible one. Constancy scaling phenomena aside, we can presumably make the judgment that a one inch long object has the same visual extension as a one foot object that is twelve times as far away.

Let us assume for a moment that we could so refine our ability to judge equivalent visual extensions that we would be able to make rapid, fairly accurate judgments about the degrees of visual field occupied by a given visual extension. Our judgments of degrees would be based, of course, on a standardly adopted unit for degrees. Berkeley's argument can now be turned around to show that tangible extension has no "determinate greatness" and so cannot be the object of geometry. That is, different visible extensions, measured by our new procedure, can be associated with the same tangible extension. According to Berkeley's original argument, this would show that the tangible extension is not of "determinate greatness."

In short, Berkeley's argument for point (b) does not establish point (b), let alone what would be needed to establish the Strong Negative Thesis, namely that visible extension cannot be assigned to a determinate metric. Rather, Berkeley's argument establishes that visible extensions can be made "determinate" and can be mapped in various ways to tangible extensions. In spite of these problems with Berkeley's argument, it does contain implicitly the claim that we must be able to assign a determinate magnitude to something if it is to be a possible object of geometry. That is, for a space to be the object of geometry, it must have a well-defined metric.

As I show in Chapter I, Reid provides the basis for just such a metric for his geometry of visibles when he introduces the relation "position with regard to the eye" in his chapter "Of Visible Figure and Extension."[10] We can use this relation to give us a measure of difference of position. The angle formed at the center (focal point) of the eye by rays projected from points having different positions with regard to the eye is a measure of difference of position: "this difference of position is greater or less, in proportion to the angle made at the eye by the right line mentioned."[11] Although Reid does not explicitly reintroduce this relation, which provides us with a metric, in his chapter on the geometry of visibles, he appeals to its use. So it will be safe for us to assume that Reid intends this method of determining distance between visible points to be a feature of the construction in the geometry of visibles.[12] The metric Reid specifies is isomorphic to the metric for a unit sphere, and so it obviously satisfies the standard axioms for "distance." So much for Berkeley's argument (b).

If Berkeley's point (c), that we always measure by applying tangible extensions to tangible extension, were to be used to establish the Strong Negative Thesis, it would have to assert that no metric, like the one just described in discussing point (b), *could* be set up for visible space. But Berkeley's argument for (c) is nothing more than the claim that our standard procedures for measuring are based on the adoption of some tangible object as a unit. Nothing in his claim rules out adopting a metric for visible space. Consider, however, a reduced claim Berkeley might try to make. He might argue that any metric we could adopt for visible space would ultimately be derivative from measurings made "by the application of tangible extension to tangible extension." Regardless of the details of any such reduced claim, it will not help Berkeley establish the Strong Negative Thesis that visible figure and extension are not the kinds of things that can be objects of geometrical study. In fact, it would really establish the Weak Negative Thesis, which Berkeley would not want for the reasons we have already discussed.

In sum, then, none of Berkeley's points (a)-(c), nor obvious modifications of his arguments for them, gives any support to the Strong Negative Thesis. One is almost led to think Berkeley conflated the clearly incompatible Strong and Weak Negative Theses. If he has done anything in his arguments for (a)-(c), it is to suggest what would be necessary to establish the Weak Negative Thesis, namely to provide a metric for visible space. And that is just what Reid provides in setting up his geometry of visibles.

The second stage of Berkeley's argument is less important than the first, and I will be briefer in describing both it and Reid's responses to it. The second stage is advanced as a "fuller illustration" of the arguments and conclusions of the first stage and consists of a thought experiment. We are asked in Section 153 of *New Theory of Vision* to "consider the case of an intelligence, or unbodied spirit, which is supposed to see perfectly well, e.g., to have a clear perception of the proper and immediate objects of sight but to have no sense of touch." Our task is to "examine what proficiency such a one may be able to make in geometry," and if we do our job correctly, we will have a clearer idea "whether the ideas of sight can possibly be the object of that science."[13] In a parallel passage, Reid asks us to suppose "a being endued with sight only, without any other external sense, and capable of reflecting and reasoning upon what he sees." We must then "conceive, as well as we can, what notion he would have of visible objects, and what conclusions he would deduce from them."[14]

Without even looking at the details of Berkeley's thought experiment, we should see that the whole thing is not directed to the point. Remember, Berkeley must establish the Strong Negative Thesis; he must show that no geometry of visible space is possible. It is not enough for him to show that a geometry of visible space must be "derivative" from a sense of touch. Unfortunately, however, he can at best establish the following claim in his thought experiment: if a being has no sense of touch, then it cannot develop a geometry (either of tangible or visible space). But such a result is still very far from proving that even if one does have a sense of touch then no geometry of visible space can be developed. At best, Berkeley's desired result, if it were true, would be of some interest to the 18th-century cognitive-psychologist—epistemologist, for it could be part of an argument to show that the sense of touch was more basic or important than the sense of vision.[15]

Reid also asks us to engage in the same thought experiment, but in his case, if we get the positive result that the touchless "being" can develop a geometry of visible space, then Reid has succeeded in giving evidence that the Weak Negative Thesis is true. The evidence would be in the form of a being whose experience "confirmed" a two-dimensional, non-Euclidean geometry. So his thought experiment, in contrast to Berkeley's, can give support to the point he is trying to make, that there is a consistent geometry of visible space. Still, Reid did not need to make his hypothetical being, the Idomenian, touchless to make his point. The reason for his doing so must lie in the attempt to respond in the most direct terms to the second stage of Berkeley's argument.

In his thought experiment Berkeley wants to establish the following five points:

(d) The intelligence will not know solid geometry.

(e) The intelligence will not know the elements of plane geometry.

(f) The intelligence might not even be able to form the idea of a geometrical plane.

(g) The immediate objects of sight are neither planes nor solids.

(h) Even if it were possible to compute the magnitude of objects of sight, there would be no point to it.

The last point, (h), is obviously not a strong one for Berkeley to make, since it is equivalent to saying that if the Weak Negative Thesis were true, it would be unimportant. The uses to which Reid puts his geometry of visibles in elaborating and modifying the theses of heterogeneity and natural signs can be seen as a direct response to point (h).

The points (d)-(g) all depend directly on a feature of Berkeley's and Reid's theories of vision I discuss in Chapter II, that we do not, strictly speaking, "see" distance. According to their theories, if we do not "see" distance, but we do make visual distance discriminations, it can only be because we have learned to coordinate visual information with information about distance coming from the sense of touch. Consequently, a touchless being would not make visual distance discriminations. Both Berkeley and Reid conclude from this that the touchless being could have no concept of distance or of three-dimensional space. As Berkeley puts it, "it is certain the afore-said intelligence could have no idea of a solid, or a quantity of three-dimensions, which followeth from its not having any idea of distance."[16] Reid agrees: "He might perceive visible objects to have length and breadth, but could have no notion of a third dimension, any more than we can have of a fourth."[17] Consequently, Reid agrees with Berkeley on points (d), (f) and (g) and goes into great detail elaborating them.[18] These agreements are, then, no threat to the geometry of visibles.

If there is any difference at all between Berkeley and Reid it will be on point (e), that the intelligence will not know the elements of plane geometry. Berkeley's arguments for (e) consist in asserting, (i) that touch is needed in order to use rulers and compasses, and (ii) that we presuppose a third dimension in all demonstrations that involve rotation of figures through a plane (say, in proving congruence).[19] Presumably, the metric for visible space that Reid provides is an answer to any non-trivial point made in (i). With regard to (ii), Berkeley has not bothered to prove that such rotations cannot always be eliminated from demonstrations. Even if some version of the point made by (ii) could be established, there is still no support forthcoming for what Berkeley needs to prove, namely the Strong Negative Thesis that objects of vision cannot be objects of geometrical study. It is exactly at this point that the thought experiment becomes irrelevant to what Berkeley really needs, for all that can be established by it is that the "idea" of a third dimension is required if one is to set up even a two-dimensional geometry and carry out demonstrations in it. But that such an "idea" is in this sense presupposed can at best show that Reid's hypothetical Idomenian is not sufficiently equipped to develop the geometry, not that no such geometry can be developed. Further, the Idomenian, once equipped with the extra "idea," would provide a model for a being whose experience was of a two-dimensional, non-Euclidean visual space. This model is all Reid needs to give further support to the Weak Negative Thesis that the visibles can be made into objects of geometrical study, even if they are not ordinarily treated as such. He does not need to prove that the geometry is "derivable" from sight alone.

Reid's non-Euclidean geometry of visibles did not, after all, come from nowhere. Reid is motivated to answer Berkeley's question about the object of geometry because he wants to refute Berkeley's idealism with regard to objects of vision. The details of Reid's exposition—especially the elaborate speculation about touchless beings—parallel Berkeley's and reflect a close reading of Berkeley's argument. What is more, the only significance Reid attributes to his discovery is that it shows exactly the sense in which visibles and tangibles are "distinct and heterogeneous": they have different geometries. No wonder, then, Reid's geometry was not recognized by his followers for what it was and was viewed as a minor elaboration in a quarrel with Berkeley. But, as I show in the next chapter, this specific origin of the geometry is only part of the story. The full explanation of Reid's desire to show that the visibles were objects of mathematical study leads us to his central arguments attacking the Ideal System and its theory of concept formation.

Chapter IV:

Reid and the 'Ideal System'

1. *The 'Ideal System'*

Reid's main goal in the *Inquiry* is to attack the Ideal System, the theory of mind advanced in the tradition leading from Descartes to Berkeley and Hume. Reid argues that once the Ideal System is accepted, one is thrown into skepticism about so many truths that something has to be wrong with the basic tenets of the system. His arguments about extension and figure are intended to serve as an *"experimentum crucis,"*[1] a crucial test of the theory of concept formation found at the core of the Ideal System. In subsequent sections I show how Reid sets up this crucial test and what its connection is to the geometry of visibles. First, however, I shall characterize the Ideal System. I cannot undertake a full explication of 18th-century theory of mind without going too far afield. Instead, I restrict the discussion to those features Reid himself picks out as central since his arguments are aimed at them.

Reid isolates the following "hypothesis" as one of two central tenets of the Ideal System:

> H1: "[T]he mind, like a mirror, receives the images of things from without, by means of the senses: so that their use must be to convey these images into the mind."[2]

Unfortunately this formulation of the hypothesis is rather vague and incomplete. It becomes clear from Reid's discussion of H1, however, that the theorist who holds it is committed at least to the following two claims. The first is an epistemological point, part of an effort to explain how concepts can apply to features of the world. The claim is that if a concept, for example the concept of red, is to apply to a feature of the world, redness, then the concept must resemble the feature. More exactly, a necessary condition for a person to have a concept that applies to a feature of the world is that he have a mental entity (the concept) structured so that it bears a resembling relation to the feature of the external world. The second claim implicit in H1 is part of a theory of concept formation: the senses are the mechanism for achieving the necessary structuring of mental entities. As Reid puts it,

> [N]o material thing, nor any quality of material things, can be conceived by us or made an object of thought, until its image is conveyed to the mind by means of the senses.[3]

In other words, Reid makes it explicit that the mechanism for producing mental entities (concepts) resembling features of the world is a necessary part of the concept formation process.

It should be noted that Reid—or at least my reading of Reid—may be slightly unfair to Berkeley or Hume here. Berkeley's "notions," for example, might be viewed by some scholars as concepts which need not bear a resembling relation to the "images" that produce them even if the "images" (sensations) are still thought necessary to the process of producing "notions." That is, this qualification would reject Reid's attribution of the first, epistemological or semantical claim to the Ideal System, but still accept his attribution of the second claim.

Although there may be textual evidence to support this objection to Reid's view of Berkeley and Hume, I think Reid has a strong point when he attributes to the Ideal System the view that concepts, and not just sensations, "resemble" real qualities. If concepts resemble sensations, which in turn resemble real qualities, then at least we are given an attempt at an explanation of how a given concept comes to apply to a given feature of the world (even if today we tend to reject this type of explanation). If we say, on the other hand, that concepts do not resemble sensations or real qualities, then we are still owed an explanation how a given concept applies to a given feature. There is not much point left in insisting that the sensation that produces the concept resembles the real quality once we drop the claim that concepts resemble features. The whole point of talking about resemblance between sensations and qualities drops out if it is removed from the context of any attempt to explain how concepts apply to features of the world.

But assume that the suggested qualification on Reid's interpretation of the Ideal System is correct. That is, assume I should exempt concepts from the resembling relation while at the same time I adopt the Ideal System's process of concept formation and insist that sensations resembling real qualities are what produce concepts. Then I believe the qualification does not save Berkeley and Hume from Reid's main criticism anyway, since Reid mainly attacks the process of concept formation proposed by the Ideal System and only secondarily its (supposed) theory about how concepts apply to features of the world. Undermining the theory of concept formation found in the Ideal System leaves these "notions" quite unsupported since we no longer know how they are formed or why they apply. It should not surprise us too much that Reid's attack on the psychological part of the theory, the concept formation hypothesis, undermines the philosophical part of it, the concept-application hypothesis: the two were intended to work together as a unified theory. As I show, Reid's attack on the theory of concept formation leads him to challenge the view that concepts apply to features only if they resemble them.

A direct corollary of these two claims about resemblance and concept formation is elevated to a principle of great importance by proponents of the Ideal System:

Corollary: "[T]o every quality or attribute of body we know or can conceive, there should be a sensation *corresponding,* which is the image or resemblance of that quality."[4] (emphasis added)

This corollary has a dual function in the Ideal System. On the one hand, it is advanced as a testable hypothesis asserting that sensations of a particular sort should be found for every case of a concept which applies to the external world. On the other hand, if we take the corollary to be well-established, then it may be used as the basis for what Reid calls a "tribunal or inquisition." Ideas (concepts) are tried before this tribunal to determine whether or not they have any real application to the external world. Ideas (concepts) for which there are no corresponding impressions (sensations) are "sentenced to pass out of existence, and to be, in all time to come, an empty unmeaning sound, or the ghost of a departed entity."[5]

Reid complains that this corollary, although such a central thesis of the "ideal system", was "so universally received by philosophers, that it was thought to need no proof."[6] Obviously, Reid is not satisfied with Hume's effort to establish his version of the corollary in the opening pages of *The Treatise*. Reid's main attack on the ideal system is an attack on the corollary. His "crucial test" is a series of arguments intended to show that the mechanism of concept formation proposed in H1 cannot account for our having the concepts of extension, figure, and motion (see Section 3 of this chapter). Specifically, Reid argues that we cannot find the appropriate resembling sensations required by the corollary. He argues that having sensations of extension and figure is neither a necessary nor a sufficient condition for having or applying concepts of these qualities. If there are such major exceptions to the corollary as extension and figure, then the Ideal System's theory of concept formation must be rejected.

The second major tenet of the Ideal System is the result, Reid claims, of arguments developed by Locke and Berkeley:

> H2: "|O|ur sensations are not images of matter, or of any of its qualities."[7]

Another formulation of H2 is the claim that "none of . . . |our sensations| . . . can in the least resemble the qualities of a lifeless and insentient being, such as matter is conceived to be."[8] Apparently, Reid takes the relations "is an image of" and "resembles" as equivalent.

It would take us aside from our purpose to explain in any detail just what H2 means or why Reid thinks it is true. In his discussions of H2 in the *Inquiry*, Chapter VI, Section VI, Reid seems to think that the various arguments from illusion, arguments from the relativity of the perceiver, and similar arguments offered by Descartes, Locke, and Malebranche establish H2 for the case of secondary qualities and corresponding sensations. Berkeley extended these arguments to primary qualities and so extended H2 as well. Unfortunately, Reid gives no explanation of the way in which those arguments are supposed to establish H2 (and we shall not try to help him). Rather, Reid seems to fall back on a sledgehammer "argument" offered by Berkeley: namely, that nothing is "like" an idea except an idea.

It is difficult to see, however, why Reid finds Berkeley's argument at all convincing. What theory lurks behind the claim that a mental image cannot resemble a material object just because one is mental substance and the other material? If "like" is taken to mean "is identical with," then of course Berkeley is right. But "like" is supposed to mean the same as "resembles," not "is identical with." If Reid means something so obvious as the argument that a mental image of an object would have to be extended to be an image of an extended object, and consequently could not be *mental*, then he would say so. If "likeness" means only "likeness of essence," Reid should say so. Reid gives us no help.

We might attempt to give an alternative argument for the claim that "nothing is like an idea but an idea," although it does not address itself to the special question of sentient vs. insentient substances which Reid sometimes treats as the key to the claim. Let us set aside the possible objection that Berkeley's "notions" may not be images, and assume that ideas (concepts) are mental images. Then, to have an idea of something is to have a mental image of it. But a mental image of Berkeley and a mental image of a mental image of Berkeley can have identical distributions of color patches. This would mean, however, that my idea of Berkeley (my mental image of

Berkeley) is identical with my idea of an idea of Berkeley (my mental image of a mental image of Berkeley) which is something other than, something distinct from, an idea of an idea of Berkeley. But then, the idealist can ask, if in fact I can have no idea of Berkeley distinct from an idea of Berkeley, then how can I claim that there is such a thing as Berkeley distinct from, but resembling, an idea of Berkeley? In other words, since I can have no idea of anything "like" an idea of Berkeley other than another idea of Berkeley, it makes no sense to say there is something like an idea of Berkeley which is not an idea of Berkeley.[9]

It would take me too far afield to assess in detail this alternative argument. What is important to note is that *it relies heavily on the mistaken analysis in H1 that concepts are mental phenomena of the same type as images.* Also, it assumes that visual images are no more than color patches, rather than, say, the Gestaltist "image-plus-set." In any case, it does not help us to understand why Reid, the anti-idealist, would support H2, the claim that sensations do not resemble qualities. On this alternative argument the reason that H2 is true is that it makes no sense to say that there are qualities, and so, obviously, sensations will not resemble qualities! Reid cannot accept this reason for believing H2: he thinks there are qualities and he argues that qualities are distinct from sensations. It seems that we must settle for the fact that Reid thinks H2 is true even if we do not know why he does. Perhaps Reid gives us no help here because he is mainly interested in showing that sensations play little, if any, role in concept formation, a result which renders the first hypotheses (H1) false and the second (H2) irrelevant.

As far as Reid is concerned, H1 and H2 are the central tenets of the Ideal System. Their conjunction is the feature of the Ideal System that most worries him, for it seems to lead to extreme skepticism. By attacking the double claim (H1) that concepts are mental entities resembling the things they are concepts of and that sensations produce concepts, Reid intends to destroy the Ideal System and the skepticism that he thinks follows from it.

2. *The Strategy of Reid's attack on the Ideal System*

The Hypotheses H1 and H2, which form the central tenets of the Ideal System on Reid's analysis, give rise to the following skeptical argument:

(i) We have no sensation of color resembling any quality of body. (Instance of H2)

(ii) We have a concept of color and color is a quality of bodies only if we have sensation of color resembling that quality. (Instance of Corollary to Hypothesis One)[10]

therefore, the *reductio:*

(iii) We have a concept of color only if color is not a quality of bodies.

(iv) We have a concept of color.

(v) Colors are not qualities of bodies.

Remember that the point of H1 is in part to explain how concepts which purport to apply to the external world arise. But the conjunction of H1 and H2 leads to (v), which seems to imply that the concept of color does not, after all, apply to the external world. To predicate "color" of a body cannot mean, as a result of (i)-(v), that the external body has some particular "fixed and permanent" quality. Since H2 is intended to encompass all sensations and all qualities of bodies, then arguments analogous to (i)-(v) will lead us to conclude that none of the concepts we have are concepts applying to real qualities of bodies. H1 has the intention of explaining how concepts which purport to apply to features of the external world are produced and can so apply. But it has the consequence, when combined with H2, that there are no such concepts at all! At this point the idealist will try to save the concepts by denying there are real features of the external world to which they can apply.[11] That is, we are only a short step from the idealist conclusion that there are no real qualities of bodies, or, as Reid puts it, "there is nothing existing in nature but . . . ideas."[12] Of course, Reid thinks that our concepts that purport to refer to real qualities *do* so and he is thus driven to his nativism, as I show in Chapter V, in order to provide a different concept formation process from that proposed in the Ideal System.

Reid's strategy for attacking this skeptical argument is to convert the argument (i)-(v), and analogues to it, into a *reductio ad absurdum* with the intention of rejecting the premise (ii) and its analogues. To accomplish this goal, Reid tries to establish the following claim:

(o) Color is a real quality of bodies.

If (o) is a premise, alone with (i), (ii), and (iv), then the contradiction between (v) and (o) should lead us to challenge at least one of (i), (ii), or (iv). But we have seen that Reid accepts (i), since he thinks no sensations resemble qualities (H2) (although we are not sure why). Further, no one wanted to reject (iv), the elementary claim that we have a concept of color! So (ii), the instance of H1, must be false. But the negation of (ii) is:

(vi) We have a concept of color and color is a quality of bodies and we have no sensation of color resembling that quality.

This conclusion, (vi), is a counterexample to H1 and its corollary. It should also be clear that this *reductio* strategy will work equally well for the case of "sound," "heat," "figure," or "extension," instead of "color," and, so, many counterexamples to the corollary can be generated. Before seeing how Reid argues in the cases central to our interest, "figure" and "extension," I shall look briefly at his handling of the case of "color."

How, then, does Reid argue for premise (o), that color is a real quality of bodies? In an argument sometimes cited as a precursor of 20th-century ordinary language arguments, which we might call the Argument from Common

Knowledge, Reid tries to show that the common usage of the
term "color" requires that the term denote a real quality of
bodies and not a sensation. For example, Reid argues that no
one thinks the color of a red body has changed just because we
look at it through green glasses.[13] Other examples are given to
show that we commonly believe, and reflect this belief in our
language, that "red" denotes a quality of body which is the
cause of the special sensation we have on seeing red bodies. In
answer to the objection that we cannot have knowledge of a
cause if we know it only through its effects, and "therefore"
there can be no such cause, Reid answers that we know many
qualities of body only through their effects. He cites gravity,
magnetism, and narcotics as examples.[14] In short, the
distinction we mark in our language between different kinds
of things, "sensations" and "qualities," marks a real distinction in the world: "there is really a permanent quality of
body, to which the common use of this word |color| exactly
agrees. Can any stronger proof be desired, that this quality is
that to which the vulgar give the name of *color?*"[15]

Reid's proof of (o), the claim that color is a real quality of
bodies, amounts, then, to the claim that realism, and not
idealism, is compatible with the ways in which non-
philosophers think and talk about colors, both in normal and
scientific discourse. This claim is hardly a proof of realism.
Rather, it functions as a warning that so well entrenched a
theory as realism is not to be abandoned unless the idealist has
some overwhelming arguments on his side. Reid's "crucial
test" (see next section) shows that there are no such arguments
for the Ideal System.

In addition to arguing for premise (o), Reid also contends
in the Argument from Common Knowledge that the idealist,
such as Berkeley, is an equivocator. The Argument shows,
Reid says, that it is "an abuse of language" for the idealist to
claim that "red" denotes a sensation rather than what
everyone uses it to denote, a quality of bodies:

> The vulgar have undoubted right to give names to things
> which they are daily conversant about; and philosophers

> seem justly chargeable with an abuse of language, when
> they change the meaning of a common word, without
> giving warning.[16]

This attack is an attempt to hit the idealist right where it
hurts—at the point at which he tries to avoid skepticism by
resorting to idealism. In the argument (i)-(v) above, I noted
the paradoxical conclusion that a theory intended to explain
how we derive concepts that purport to apply to features of
the external world seems instead to force us to conclude that
there are no such concepts at all! The real world seems to fall
out from under the concepts we think apply to it. In order to
reassure us against any sense of loss, the idealist tries to
convince us that terms like "color," "heat," "sound," and the
like always denote only sensations and not qualities. He tries
to convince us that we lose nothing, since we cannot lose what
in fact we never in reality talk or think about. Reid, on the
other hand, insists that this attempt at reassurance is really
only an equivocation. If skepticism is to be avoided, we shall
have to eliminate premise (ii), the claim that we have a concept
of color and that color is a quality of bodies only if we have
sensations of color resembling that quality.

The main thrust of Reid's attack on the "ideal system," in
particular on the double claim (H1) that concepts are mental
entities resembling the thing they are concepts of and that
sensations produce concepts, comes in the case of figure and
extension, not secondary qualities like color. In the case of
figure and extension a *reductio* strategy like that outlined for
secondary qualities still lies in the background of Reid's
argument, but Reid does not make it as prominent. For
example, he does not even pretend to argue, as he does in the
case of color, that extension is a quality of bodies; that is, he
really assumes, as part of his realist stance, that

  (o′) extension is a quality of bodies.

Of course, if Reid is granted this assumption (o′), then he can
carry out an analogous *reductio* to (o′)-(vi′). But Reid does not

rest content with this indirect argument and instead makes a more direct attack on the theory of concept formation contained in the Ideal System.

Reid tries, as we shall see in the next section, to establish the following claim:

(NSS): We have no special sensations of extension.

Before explaining just what is meant by saying "there is no *special* sensation of extension," we shall first ask why Reid wants to establish (NSS) rather than simply use the *reductio* (o')-(vi'). The answer lies in Reid's desire to counter a special move made by the idealist. The idealist, as I show, tries to convince us that the concepts we thought applied to external features of the world, like color, in fact apply only to sensations. The idealist shifts the psychological thesis that our concepts are derived from resembling mental entities, namely sensations, to the claim that our concepts not only *derive* from, but also *apply* only to those sensations, and not to any external features of the world. If the idealist does not make this move, then what is to stop the concept from being hauled up before the "tribunal" established by the corollary to H1 and "sentenced to pass out of existence, and to be . . . the ghost of a departed entity?"[17] Since the idealist can no longer claim that the concept applies to features of the external world, he has to find something to which it applies or else he has to stop calling it a concept and has to reduce it instead to the status of a "fiction." Berkeley's equivocation, which we have just seen Reid attack, is intended to save concepts from this fate.

If, however, Reid can show that there is no "special" sensation corresponding to our concept of extension, then the idealist's effort to save the concept of extension from the fate of fictions is in real jeopardy. If there is neither a real, external quality which "extension" denotes, nor a special sensation corresponding to the concept "extension," then either there is no concept of extension but only a fiction, or else the concept of extension does not apply to any resembling sensation. The idealist can afford neither consequence of Reid's attack on the process of concept formation in the Ideal System. The former is incompatible with the commonly accepted legitimacy of the important concept "extension." The latter directly contradicts the idealist's attempt to "save" the concepts by claiming they *apply* to sensations rather than qualities.

Reid can offer an alternative theory of concept formation compatible with (NSS), the claim that we have no special sensations of extension. In his discussion of visible figure and extension, he claims that our concepts may be "suggested" by physical impressions on our sense organs. He simply says that certain physical interactions with our environment "suggest" concepts as a consequence of the way in which we are put together, "by our constitution." Sometimes this alternative mechanism tempts Reid into upholding the old analysis of "having a concept" contained in the Ideal System, namely, having a mental entity bearing structural resemblance to features of the external world. But there is a problem here. In our discussion of Reid's reasons for holding H2, the claim that no sensations resemble qualities, I suggested he has no reason other than Berkeley's sledge-hammer argument that no mental entity can be "like" any material entity. Consequently, concepts, just like sensations, cannot resemble qualities of bodies, contrary to the analysis contained in the Ideal System. So we should expect Reid to try to avoid relying on that analysis.

Indeed, Reid does try to edge himself away from the analysis of "having a concept" put forward in the Ideal System. He at times seems to substitute for it the view that "having a concept" should better be understood as having a certain complex set of abilities. In a key argument about visible figure, Reid claims that if we can attribute certain abilities to someone, that is sufficient grounds for claiming he has a certain concept. This analysis goes directly against the one which supports the corollary to H1. The Corollary requires us to exhibit an appropriate (conscious) sensation which can give rise to a given concept before we can say someone has that concept. But by (NSS), there is no such sensation in the case of extension. Reid is here on the verge of plunging sensations into an insignificant role in our theories of mind and knowledge—even if he offers no well developed alternative.

3. *The 'Crucial Test': Arguments about Sensation*

In the remainder of our discussion of Reid's attack on the Ideal System we shall discuss four central arguments about figure and extension. The first two arguments, The Argument for No Special Sensation and the Argument for the Independence of Color and Figure, form a pair which establish the claim that we have no special sensations of extension (NSS), first for touch and then for vision. The third argument is a thought experiment intended to show that no introspectible tactile sensations we have are sufficient to produce the concepts of figure and extension. The fourth argument, The Argument from the Blind Mathematician, not only strengthens support for (NSS) but also elaborates Reid's attack on the traditional analysis of "having a concept." But most importantly, The Argument from the Blind Mathematician contains the main ideas present in the geometry of visibles and so forms the link between Reid's main interest in the *Inquiry,* attacking the Ideal System of mind, and my contention that Reid's discovery of a non-Euclidean geometry is rooted in his case for realism.

The Argument for No Special Sensation, which must be assembled from a series of points scattered throughout Reid's discussion of touch, is intended to establish the analogue of (NSS) for all primary qualities. In order to state the Argument properly I have to explain Reid's version of the distinction between primary and secondary qualities. First, he claims that there is a major difference between the understanding we have of what primary and secondary qualities are: we have "clear and distinct" conceptions of the former but not of the latter. Second, because of this difference in our understanding of the nature of these two kinds of qualities, the sensations which may correspond to each kind play different roles in our ability to apply the respective concepts. I show that Reid ties our "conceptions" of secondary qualities more closely to sensations than he does our conceptions of primary qualities, even though, of course, no sensations resemble qualities.

I begin by trying to explain Reid's claim that we have no "clear and distinct" conception of secondary qualities like red. The term "red" denotes a quality, say r, of bodies. We do not know, however, exactly what r is. We have only a "relative" conception of r: we treat r as an unknown cause of a known effect, namely, as the unknown cause of a given sensation, Sr, "the appearance of red." So our conception of red is not clear, since we do not know exactly what it is ("unknown cause"); and it is not distinct, since we can distinguish red from blue only by reference to the sensations they produce in us ("known effect").

It is apparent from various passages in the *Inquiry* that although Reid sometimes refers to r as a "power" he really thinks scientists will discover that r is some structural property of bodies. In fact, it is the job of the natural sciences to discover just what structural property of bodies is denoted by "red." Thus for secondary qualities, but not, as we shall see, for primary qualities, it is appropriate for scientists to formulate hypotheses of the form: red is such and such a physicochemical property of bodies.[18] Such hypotheses about r are an attempt to identify the cause of Sr. If correct, they could result in a clear and distinct conception of red.

Because scientists do not yet have theories which permit us to identify secondary qualities, the sensations produced by such qualities, like Sr, play a necessary role in helping us to distinguish one such quality from another. Even if scientists did develop such theories, unless the ordinary language user could make the identifications and distinctions the scientist does, then the theoretical advance would not affect the general point about the role of sensations in these cases. Reid explains that role in this way:

> When we think or speak of any particular color, however simple the notion may seem to be, which is presented to

the imagination, it is really in some sort compounded. It involves an unknown cause, and a known effect. The name of *color* belongs indeed to the cause only, and not to the effect. But as the cause is unknown, we can form no distinct conception of it, but by its relation to the known effect . . . I must therefore, for the sake of distinction, join to each of them, in my imagination, some effect or some relation that is peculiar. And the most obvious distinction is, the appearance which one and the other makes to the eye.[19]

The following thought experiment helps draw out some of the implications of Reid's account of secondary quality terms. Assume we live in a world which consists only of beach balls, half of which are red and half blue. Let "red" denote the unknown quality r of beach balls, and let "blue" denote unknown quality b of beach balls. Further, let us assume that at the time T_1, r has effect S_1 in the entire population, that is, it produces sensation S_1 in everyone. Assume also that at T_1 b produces S_2 in half the population although it produces S_3 in the other half.[20] Then, the whole population has the same conception or "notion," n_1 of red: "the unknown quality causing S_1." Half the population has one notion, n_2, of blue: "the unknown quality causing S_2." The other half has notion n_3 of blue: "the unknown quality causing S_3." The two notions (we might call them "connotations") n_2 and n_3 produce complete agreement in use of the term "blue"; they are two different ways of picking out the referrent or denotation of "blue." It seems, then, that uniformity in denotation, not connotation suffices to have the term "blue" function properly as a color word.

Now let us suppose that half the population, the half with S_3, suddenly finds at time T_2 that it wants to call all beach balls "blue" which are called "red" by the other half of the population (the half with S_2), and that it wants to call "red" all beach balls called "blue" by the other half. This might happen as a result of a sudden change in the laws of psychophysics. That is, at T_2 r causes S_3 instead of S_1 and b causes S_1 whenever a perceiver has S_3 rather than S_2; but the laws remain as before whenever a perceiver has S_2 instead of S_3. At T_2, the half of the population with S_2 still uses n_2 to pick out b and n_1 to pick out r. But the other half of the population uses n_1 to pick out b and n_3 to pick out r. Neither half of the population can know whether it is the one that has deviated from previous usage since there had been no way to identify r and b independently of using n_1, n_2, and n_3. There had been no "clear and distinct" notions of red and blue but only "relative" notions.

In this situation, in order to reestablish a uniform usage of "blue" and "red," the usage of one half of the population would have to be arbitrarily accepted as standard, say by a "linguistic convention," and the other half would have to be retrained. The retrained half would have to switch the notions it associates with the terms "red" and "blue." But switching these notions in accord with an arbitrary agreement means nothing more than switching which sensation is used to pick out the denotation of "red" and "blue," making our notion "relative" to a different sensation. We can put this another way. Our notion or conception of red or blue is *semantically tied* to a given sensation if and only if there is not a way to reestablish uniform usage of "red" and "blue" other than by resorting to an arbitrary convention, as in the thought experiment just described. The reason such semantically tied sensations are needed here is that there is no "clear and distinct" conception or notion of the quality that would permit us to identify it independently of associated sensations, but only a "relative" conception that forces us to appeal to the sensation. We can call such semantically tied sensations *special sensations.* All secondary qualities have these special sensations corresponding to them.

The case is different, on our interpretation of Reid, for primary qualities like hardness, softness, smoothness, and roughness, as well as for a second group of primary qualities, extension, figure, and motion. Let us concentrate on the former group, with hardness as a particular example. Whereas we have no "clear and distinct" concept of the color quality red, but only the "relative" conception, "unknown quality causing Sr," we do have a clear and distinct concept of the quality of body denoted by "hardness." Reid gives two formulations of our conception of hardness: hardness is "|t|he cohesion of the parts of a body, with more or less force,"[21] or the "adherence" of the parts . . . of a body so firm that it can not easily be made to change its figure."[22] The latter formulation includes rigidity in the concept of hardness. Not only can we actually give such descriptions of primary qualities, but we can do so using only the most basic notions from physics (force) and geometry (figure, or "the relation of parts one to another"). Each of these primary qualities is described, then, by a part of a very elementary theory of the properties of bodies. The "concept" of these qualities are part of the apparatus of a primitive mechanics widely known to all language users.

Since we already possess primitive mechanics and thus know what primary qualities are and how they are related to one another, it is not a proper inquiry for scientists to ask, "what hardness in bodies is."[23] That is, hypotheses analogous to those offered about color would be "ridiculous." On the other hand it is proper for scientists to try to *explain* why a body has the property of hardness, why the parts of bodies cohere with different degrees of force, say, by giving an adequate theory of the forces involved in molecular bonding or crystalline structures. With colors, we do not even know what the quality is, let alone have explanations about why it is what it is.

The main problem with Reid's claim that we have "clear and distinct" concepts of primary, but not of secondary qualities is that Reid assumes he is pointing out a special feature of the *concepts themselves*, rather than a feature they may have *relative* to the common theories we have of bodies. There are many questions I can but will not raise about Reid's version of the primary-secondary quality distinction. Other philosophers have also tried to explain the distinction by reference to the degree to which primary qualities are tied to our basic beliefs about bodies or substance. We need not go into these matters here.

Let us carry out a thought experiment like the one for secondary qualities to see why having a "clear and distinct" concept of hardness is of importance. This time let h and s be the qualities of our beach balls denoted by "hard" and "soft" respectively. Assume a similar split in the population. That is, at T_1 h causes S_1 in the whole population, and s causes S_2 in half the population, but s causes S_3 in the other half. Everyone, however, has a clear and distinct conception of hardness, n_1: "the strong adherence of the parts of the body so that it does not change its figure easily." With this notion, n_1, there is associated the sensation S_1, but reference to S_1 is not made in the statement of our conception of hardness. Similarly, the whole population will have the following notion of softness, n_2: "weak adherence of the parts of the body so that it does change its figure easily." But half the population associates S_2 with n_2 and half associates S_3 with n_2. Let us suppose that at T_2, in the population having S_3, h causes S_3 instead of S_1 and s causes S_1 instead of S_3; everything is as at T_1 for the rest of the population. Will there be the same confusion about the usage of "hard" and "soft" as there had been about "red" and "blue" at T_2? Would one need a "linguistic convention" to re-establish a uniform usage?

If our interpretation of Reid is basically correct, the answer is "no" to both questions (although this central point is not prominent in Reid's own exposition). The basic theory of bodies, our primitive mechanics, gives us various ways by means of which we can check to see which beach balls are hard (have h) and which soft (have s) at T_2, regardless of confusion in associated sensations S_1, S_2, and S_3. For example, we might apply various forces to a body to see if it changes figure easily, that is, to see if it is hard. In other words, having this body of theory, primitive mechanics, we will have open to us ways of identifying the presence of h or s independently of S_1-S_3. This is exactly what is meant by saying our conceptions of primary qualities are not "relative" to certain sensations: S_1-S_3 are not semantically tied to our conceptions of primary qualities. Consequently, these concepts of primary qualities will not have special sensations corresponding to them. The associated sensations S_1-S_3 are not special sensations.

I can now try to state the Argument for No Special Sensations in the case of the primary qualities hardness, softness, smoothness, and roughness. As in the case of secondary quality terms, terms for primary qualities denote a quality or property of bodies, not a sensation. But in contrast with the case of secondary qualities, we have notions or conceptions of primary qualities which are both clear and distinct. They are "clear" in that we can define[24] each quality in elementary theoretical language that employs only the most basic primitives from physics and geometry. They are "distinct" in that we can distinguish these qualities from one another without reference to sensations because their connection with the elementary theory of bodies gives us obvious ways of determining whether or not they are present. On the other hand, neither clarity nor distinctness was a feature of our notions or conceptions of secondary qualities. We have no *clear* conception of what the quality is, but only the notion of an unknown cause. We have no *distinct* notion of that cause, but only a relative notion, because we are able to individuate unknown causes only by appeal to their known effects. We called this close tie of the sensation caused by a secondary quality to our conception of the quality a "semantic tie," and we said that concepts of secondary qualities have corresponding to them semantically tied or *special* sensations. Primary qualities are tied to an elementary theory of bodies, common knowledge of which makes the appeal to special sensations unnecessary since it provides us with various ways of detecting primary qualities independently of any reference to sensations. Of course, the primary qualities considered so far do have sensations associated with them, which Reid says serve as "signs" for the qualities. Since these sensations are not special sensations, however, I have established the analogue of (NSS) for the case of hardness, a member of the first group of primary qualities. That is, there is no special sensation of hardness.

So far we have not considered extension, figure and motion,[25] primary qualities which Reid treats in a slightly different manner from hardness and roughness, as we shall see. They are, however, subject to the Argument for No Special Sensation, and thus we can establish (NSS) and its analogues for figure and motion. Our conceptions or notions of extension and figure are also "clear and distinct." In fact, we require even fewer primitives from what we called the "general theory of bodies" than are needed to state our conception of hardness, etc., since we can omit force and other primitives from physics. Futhermore, extension and figure are both *presupposed* by hardness, softness, and the rest of the first group, since the terms "extension" and "figure" appear in our definitions of "hardness," "roughness," etc.[26] But the clarity and distinctness of our conceptions of extension and figure are sufficient grounds for our being able to elaborate the Argument for No Special Sensation for them.

There may be a problem with Reid's claim that we have clear and distinct conceptions of figure and extension. As I show on my interpretation of Reid, a concept of a primary quality is *clear* (and distinct) because we can answer the question, "What is it?" by appealing only to certain primitives from physics and geometry. "What is hardness?" for example, was answered by appealing to "figure" and "force." But what kind of answer to the question, "What is it?" can we give for the real primitives within the elementary theory of bodies, like "position" or "force"? To be sure, we can give some circular answers, explaining what position is in terms of "figure" and "extension." But it is not at all obvious just how Reid would analyze the *clarity* of our conception of position. In other words, the clarity of certain defined but central concepts,[27] like the concept of hardness, have been explicated by showing that they can be traced back to certain clear concepts of primitives, like the concept of force and position. But there seems to be no way of explicating the clarity of our concepts of the primitives.

Reid does, of course, hold a nativist theory of concept formation for these primitives—in fact, for both primitive and defined concepts of primary qualities. He claims, as we shall see in Chapter V, that these concepts develop in accord with special laws of our constitution and are tied to "first principles," which we also have "by our constitution." He would probably hold that they are not only formed "by our constitution," but also that they are *clear* "by our constitution." This nativist theory of their formation may well commit Reid to the view that the distinction between these particular primitive and defined concepts is not theory relative, but rather is fixed for all the theories we could possibly hold. I shall discuss a related problem in Chapter V when I explain Reid's view that we develop both common (Euclidean) geometry and the (non-Euclidean) geometry of visibles "by our constitution." I conclude these objections and asides by noting that whatever new analysis of "having a concept" Reid may offer, it will apply equally well to both primitive and defined concepts of primary qualities.

The objection might also be raised that the sense which has been given to (NSS) as a result of the Argument for No Special Sensation seems to have no clear connection with our earlier description of Reid's motives for establishing (NSS) and its analogues. Earlier I suggested that (NSS), the assertion that we have no special sensation of extension, is part of Reid's attack on the idealist. The idealist claims, first, that our concept of extension applies not to a quality of body but to some corresponding sensation, and second, that our concept of extension is "derived" from and "resembles" that corresponding sensation. As a result of the Argument for No Special Sensation, however, *we find that our conception of extension would not be changed even if we altered the sensations which might be associated with that conception.*

The interconnection of primary quality concepts in an elementary mechanics frees them, in a sense, from their association with any particular sensations. But then having such sensations cannot be a necessary condition for applying the relevant concept. If having such sensations is not a necessary condition for applying the relevant concept, then

Berkeley must be wrong when he claims that our concept of hardness really applies to some corresponding touch sensations and not to a real quality. The Argument for No Special Sensation does not directly answer the claim that these concepts are "derived from" and "resemble" certain sensations. One could, for example, insist on the necessity of sensation as the mechanism for derivation and relinquish Berkeley's claim that the concepts apply to corresponding sensations and not to real qualities. Reid does not rest content with this initial victory, for, as I show, he also wants to prove that the derivation thesis is false as well.

There is still another important effect of the Argument for No Special Sensation: it suggests that we had better understand that some of our most important concepts are parts of a theory and not just isolated effects produced by special sensations. This suggestion is picked up on and developed in the Argument from the Blind Mathematician, where Reid argues that a body of theory containing a given concept *can be acquired even if the sensations which had been thought to be necessary to produce that concept are absent.* Thus the Argument for No Special Sensation sets the stage for an even sharper attack on the Ideal System, one which focuses on the thesis that having certain sensations is a necessary condition for deriving certain concepts.

Although the Argument for No Special Sensation does establish (NSS) and its analogue for figure, there is a difference between Reid's treatment of the geometrical primary qualities and his treatment of the mechanical ones. In fact, Reid is even sharper in attacking the Ideal System's theory of concept formation in the case of extension and figure than he is in the case of hardness and softness or secondary qualities. We have already noted that Reid believes the concepts of extension and figure to be the most central ones in the elementary theory of bodies, being presupposed in the definitions of the mechanical primary qualities. This conceptual point is balanced against a cognitive psychological remark which needs some explanation. Reid remarks,

[I]t must . . . be allowed, that if we had never felt
anything hard or soft, rough or smooth, . . . we should
never have had a conception of extension.[28]

I interpret Reid to mean that our concepts of figure and
extension develop on the basis of our feeling hard, soft, rough,
and smooth objects. Reid also suggests that "[e]xtension [and
figure] . . seems to be a quality suggested to us, by the very
same sensations which suggest the other qualities."[29] If I hold
a small ball in my hand, Reid says, the "very simple" feeling I
have suggests that the ball is hard, figured, and extended. But
the Ideal System requires a distinct, "resembling" sensation
for each distinct concept!

Reid seems to believe, according to the latter suggestion,
that extension and figure are not the kinds of qualities of
bodies that can, by psycho-physical laws, produce sensations
of touch in us. On the other hand, bodies do have primary
qualities of the mechanical variety, hardness, roughness, and
the like, which can produce sensations in us by psycho-
physical laws, even if these sensations are *not* semantically tied
to our conceptions of hardness, roughness, and the others, as
argued above. The figure of a body (a geometrical primary
quality), that is, the array of its boundary points, is revealed to
touch through the sensations caused by the mechanical
primary qualities of its boundary points. On this
interpretation, Reid seems to be arguing that there are no
sensations at all, distinct from the (non-special) sensations of
hardness, smoothness, etc., that are sensations of position. If
this is true, then certainly the thesis is false that distinct,
resembling sensations are a necessary precondition for
deriving concepts of figure and extension. Admittedly, this
point is an extrapolation from what Reid actually does say,
since he never quite makes this point so explicit in the case of
touch. This point, however, is made quite explicit for visual
position in the Argument for the Independence of Color and
Figure, which I now introduce.

The Argument for the Independence of Color and Figure
is intended to answer the question, "whether there be any

sensation proper to visible figure, by which it is suggested in vision?"[30] First, Reid notes that introspection gives us some evidence for a negative answer. When we see a red beach ball, we do have a definite sensation, namely, "the appearance which the color of it makes." This sensation "suggests" (Reid's favorite hedging word) "some external thing as its cause; but it suggests likewise the individual direction and position of this cause with regard to the eye."[31] Reid's key point is that, "I am not conscious of any thing that can be called a *sensation*, but the sensation of color. The position of the colored thing is *no sensation*, but it is by the laws of my constitution presented to the mind along with the color, *without any additional sensation.*"[32] Thus far the evidence parallels the situation for tactual sensations of hardness, which "suggest" extension and figure *without additional sensation.*

Reid is not satisfied with this evidence from introspection and sets up a thought experiment (The Argument for Independence) intended to show that there is nothing about the sensation of color itself that makes having it either a necessary or sufficient condition for the perception of position (and figure). We should read the argument as a direct response to Berkeley's claim that visible figure and extension are not ideas distinct from color (cf. *New Theory of Vision*, Sections 43 and 130). From the "common view" that color is "in the mind," Berkeley had argued that since visible figure and extension are not distinct from color, then visible figure and extension are also in the mind. Reid's effort to attack the claim that they are not distinct is motivated by his desire to show that visible figure and extension are "objects" external to the mind. (Cf. Chapter I, Section 2; Chapter III, Section 1). He shows this externality of visible figure *even if* color is "in the mind"; but we have already seen Reid attack the idealist move to put color "in the mind" as an idealist equivocation (cf. p. 69). These motivational remarks complete, I proceed to the argument.

We are asked first to imagine two cases of modified eyes and to speculate about what such eyes would be able to see. In

Case 1 the eye is so constituted that rays from a point object do not focus, but are diffused over the retina. Reid argues that such eyes would see the color but not the position or figure of bodies. He says extreme cataract cases meet the conditions of this modification. From this result, Reid concludes that having a sensation of color is not a sufficient condition for seeing position and figure of colored objects.

In *Case 2* we are asked to imagine that the "laws of our constitution" are altered in such a way that the material impression of light rays on retinas "suggests" only position (and figure), but not color. That is, there is no resultant sensation of color. The material impression on the retina is *not* something of which we are conscious. It is a bodily, not mental, impression. Reid argues that 18th-century theory of vision tells us nothing more than that the material impression normally "suggests," by "laws of our constitution," *both* color and position (and figure) to the eye. We do not know the mechanism. So Reid's second case is only an effort to change a particular fact about the relation between material impressions and "suggested" concepts. Such a supposition is not contradictory, for we were not from the beginning considering any (logically) necessary connection between color and figure perception. On the supposition of *Case 2,* since there is no color sensation, we would perceive visible figure without having any sensation or impression made on our mind at all. Consequently, Reid concludes that the having of a color sensation is not (logically) necessary to the perception of figure. Remember that Reid is responding to Berkeley, who said that we cannot "even in thought" "abstract" color from figure or extension.

Cases 1 and 2 are intended to establish that any connection between sensations of color and perception of figure is accidental. But then any connection in the normal eye is also accidental. Case 3 asks us to restore to the eye used in Case 2 the ability to perceive color. Reid concludes that the restored eye "perceives figure in the very same manner" as in Case 2, with this difference only, "that color is always joined with it."[33]

The heart of The Argument for Independence lies in Case 2. Actually, it is better to modify Case 2 so that Reid is arguing that visual position perception is possible not only without color sensations, but also without any light-contrast sensations. This makes the case more interesting and harder to imagine. Perhaps Reid would have liked to have on hand, as a suggestive model, an electronic position detector (say a radar-controlled automatic pilot) which clearly has no *sensations* of any kind. I will not concern myself here with any effort either to support or to attack Reid on the merits of his thought experiment.

What is of interest here is the thrust of Reid's argument: he reduces to a minimum the role played by sensations in concept formation, attacking sharply the theory of concept formation advanced in the Ideal System. Sensations seem to drop out of the picture completely in some cases. This basic thrust is explicit in Reid's own conclusion from his thought experiment:

> [T]here seems to be no sensation that is appropriated to visible figure, or whose office it is to suggest it. It seems to be suggested immediately by the material impression upon the organ, of which we are not conscious: and why may not a material impression upon the *retina* suggest visible figure, as well as the material impression made upon the hand, when we grasp a ball, suggests real figure? In the one case, one and the same material impression suggests both colour and visible figure; and in the other case, one and the same material impression suggests hardness, heat, or cold, and real figure, all at the same time.[34]

Reid even extends his point to include tangible figure. He thus justifies our own use of the Argument for Independence to make explicit Reid's view that, in the case of geometrical primary qualities, no sensations at all, let alone no special sensations, can play the role required by the Ideal System's theory of concept formation. The only note of qualification needed here is that visible figure is *not* a primary quality of bodies described in the elementary mechanics discussed above. It is, however, related to the real (tangible) figure of bodies through mathematical constructions. Thus *our conception of visible figure is also connected to a body of basic theory, a fact that makes it function more like primary qualities than secondary qualities in its relation to sensations.*

Reid undertakes one more thought experiment to strengthen even further his claim that sensations play no role like that described in the Ideal System in our formation of the concepts of figure and extension. Reid wants to lay to rest once and for all the claim that tactual sensations could really "suggest" the conceptions we have of figure and extension in just the way maintained by the theory of concept formation found in the Ideal System. Thus far Reid argues that having corresponding sensations is not a necessary condition for applying concepts of primary qualities (The Argument for No Special Sensations) and that having corresponding sensations is not a necessary condition for deriving our concepts of tactual or visible figure and extension (The Argument for Independence). Now Reid wants to show having tactual sensations is not a sufficient condition for deriving concepts of figure and extension. He argues that the tactile sensations we have available to us on the basis of introspection cannot give rise to clear and distinct conceptions. In relying on introspective evidence, Reid is trying to refute proponents of the Ideal System on their own methodological territory, for all the evidence in Hume for his version of the corollary had been based on such introspections. Thus, this thought experiment is an attempt to show that having sensations is not a *sufficient* condition for deriving a concept of a primary quality and supplements the earlier arguments that having sensations is not a *necessary* condition either.

Reid asks the reader to imagine a blind man who has been deprived of *all* conceptions that play any role in the general theory of bodies. Subject the blind man to any variety of tactual sensations—pin pricks, varying pressure from blunt bodies, objects dragged across his skin, kinaesthetic sensations from moving a limb. Still, he will not "derive" from these sensations any *clear* and *distinct* conception of primary qualities. "Common sense" may give him the *un*clear and *in*distinct conception, "unknown cause of this known sensation of a pin prick." But that conception is a far cry from our clear and distinct conceptions of primary qualities. If we judge just by the introspectible nature of such tactual sensations, there is nothing about them that can lead us to the clear and distinct conceptions of primary qualities described in the general theory of bodies. But it is just such an introspection model which Reid had found to be the paradigm at the heart of the theory of concept formation of the Ideal System. Just such a paradigm would be used to verify H1 or its corollary, which say that resembling sensations are necessary to the production of all concepts. Reid concludes that these sensations cannot be the means by which we order our experience into knowledge of bodies and their properties—*not unless we already had those central concepts.*[35] That is, Reid seems to conclude that such sensations might act as "signs" for primary qualities, but only once we already possessed the theoretical framework of the general theory of bodies, including the conceptions of the primary qualities.

We should note that this kind of an argument has a definite Kantian flavor, and it is strongly linked by Reid to his nativist view of the *a priori* (which we shall look at in Chapter V). Here I note that this thought experiment of Reid's serves as the next to the last coffin nail for the Ideal System. The last coffin nail is the Argument from the Blind Mathematician.

In the Argument from the Blind Mathematician Reid argues once again that having visual sensations is not a necessary condition for having the concept of visible figure. Thus, this Argument drives home one more point in Reid's attack on the theory of concept formation central to the Ideal System. Taken at face value, the Argument from the Blind Mathematician is just an extra argument to show that sensations are not necessary to concept formation.

However, the interest of the Argument goes beyond what it adds to Reid's arsenal against the theory of concept formation. It contains Reid's most explicit formulation of an alternative analysis of "having a concept of x," especially where "x" names a primary quality. Such an alternative is sorely needed since the traditional analysis of "having a concept of x," central to the Ideal System, was severely undermined by Reid's attacks on the theory of concept formation (H1). The analysis underlying H1 holds that a concept is a mental entity bearing structural resemblance either to sensations or to qualities. But as a result of Reid's attacks, there are no special sensations for primary quality concepts, and no corresponding sensations at all for extension and figure: so, obviously, no such relation of resemblance can hold. Reid's attacks still leave room for maintaining that some mental presentation is present when we have a concept of extension, although the presentation can resemble neither sensations nor qualities. This reduced mental presentation analysis is highly unsatisfactory from the point of view of 18th-century theory of mind. Without the resemblance hypotheses applying to such presentations, there is not even the semblance of an explanation of how these presentations are related to what they are supposed to be concepts of.

In the Argument from the Blind Mathematician Reid suggests that one can find out that someone has a certain concept if one finds out that he has a certain complex set of abilities. This suggestion directly undercuts the contention of the corollary to H1 that one can show someone has a concept only if one can show certain corresponding sensations. As I show, the key to Reid's argument is that the concept of visible figure is integrated into a body of mathematical and optical theory. One can know such a theory in spite of the fact that one has not had the sensations corresponding to each concept used in the theory. Knowing this theory gives one a variety of abilities. If one can be shown to have these abilities, then that counts as having the concept in question, even if no one has any sensations corresponding to that concept. This argument should apply as well to any concept that is intimately bound up in a body of theory which can be held independently of having some particular set of sensations. Thus, it should readily extend to include primary qualities, which are tied to the general theory of bodies. Consequently, Reid's alternative analysis can be extended from the concept of visible figure and extension to include concepts of all primary qualities. I here restrict myself to exposition of the Argument in the case of the concept of visible figure.

The Argument from the Blind Mathematician is stated twice. In Chapter VI, Section II, of the *Inquiry* Reid states it in an abridged form. He argues to the conclusion that a man born blind can have a "distinct notion, if not of the very things, ["the visible appearance of figure, and motion and extension of bodies"] at least of something extremely like to them."[36] The argument itself, however, depends on believing that one can find out if someone has a certain concept if one can verify that he has certain abilities. In this case, having the notion or conception of visible figure requires having the ability to state how the visible figures of bodies will vary depending on their relation to the eye:

> May he not be made to conceive, that a plain surface, in a certain position, may appear as a straight line, and vary its visible figure, as its position, or the position of the eye, is varied? That a circle seen obliquely will appear an ellipse; and a square, a rhombus, or an oblong rectangle; Dr. Saunderson understood the projection of the sphere, and the common rules of perspective; and if he did, he must have understood all that I have mentioned.[37]

Reid is really making several points here. First it is clear that a concept like the concept of visible figure is intricately related to a body of mathematical and optical theory. If one knows enough of this theory, one will know a great deal about the properties and behavior of the visible figure of bodies. But secondly, knowing these things about visible figure gives someone a variety of *abilities,* for example, the ability to distinguish various visible figures from one another depending on the real figure of a body and its position with regard to the eye, the ability to use correctly a whole body of sentences about visible figures, and so forth. So deciding whether or not the blind mathematician has an "adequate conception of visible figure" requires knowing whether or not he has these various abilities. Reid is fairly clear that he regards finding such abilities *sufficient* reason to claim that the blind man has an adequate conception. He expresses no interest in what sort of mental presentation might take place when the man exercises his abilities. Similarly, he ignores the possible line of objection that would grant the blind mathematician only an attenuated or truncated concept of visible figure.

These points emerge more clearly in the second, fuller statement of the Argument from the Blind Mathematician in Section VI, Chapter VI of the *Inquiry,* which I shall try to paraphrase. We do not (yet) have theories which can tell us whether or not a given color affects the eyes of different men in the same way. We do have theories of optics and vision which show that "every eye that sees distinctly and perfectly, must, in the same situation, see . . . |a given body|. . . under. . . |a given| . . . form, and no other."[38] Consequently, given the real figure, magnitude, and position of a body and an eye, we can deduce by mathematical reasoning the visible figure from the real figure. Simply set the eye in the center of a hollow sphere and project the real figure of the given body through the eye onto the sphere. But such a construction can readily be understood by a blind man knowing the appropriate mathematics. Furthermore, the blind man can readily understand two further principles: first, that the distance between two visible points will vary with the magnitude of the angles the points subtend; and second, that "the eye, until it is aided by experience, does not represent one object as nearer or more remote than another."[39] In other words, the blind man can understand and apply a metric to a two-dimensional visible space. That is, the blind man can, through mathematical construction, have the "vicarious" experience of seeing through The Eye we described in Chapter I. He can make the same discriminations.

In sum, then, we can expect the blind man to be able to describe the properties of visible figures of bodies. That is, we can expect him to have a clear and distinct conception of "the position[40] of the several parts (of a body) with regard to the eye," that is, of the visible figure of bodies; for, by analogy, all that is required for him to have a clear and distinct conception of real figure is that he have a clear and distinct conception of "the parts of the body with regard to one another." On the other hand, the blind man does not even have a "relative" conception of color, since he has no color sensations by means of which he can distinguish one color from another. Therefore, it must be possible to develop a distinct conception of visible figure independently of having any visual sensations (e.g. of colors) or of having any distinct conception of color. This, of course, is a direct attack on Berkeley, as I argue above. Finally, visible figures cannot be (identical with) visual sensations; nor can visible figures, if they are treated as "abstract mental entities," be abstractions solely from visual sensations (cf. Chapter I, Section 2). Even if the blind man "associates" his notion of visible figure with sensations of touch, whereas normal men associate their notions of visible figure with sensations of color, these different associations should not "make things seem different, which in reality are the same."[41]

The paraphrase of the full argument develops some of the points noted above. Reid tries to show that the mathematician has a variety of intricately related abilities in order to show that he has a certain concept. The mathematician, using appropriate constructions, can distinguish visible figures one from another, can know when two real figures will have the same visible figures, and the like. These abilities to distinguish visible figures from one another are substantial evidence that the mathematician *has* the concept. The nature of the thought experiment rules out any relevant sensory presentations. Visible figures are described by a body of mathematical theory. Understanding this theory—being able to use and apply it—shows one has the concept of visible figure. There is no need to hunt up any corresponding sensation.

The claim that Reid has a developed alternative analysis of "having a concept" must be strongly qualified. First, Reid does not develop the implications of his alternative analysis. Second, he does not explicitly contrast it to the dominant theory of the peroid. Third, his own language at many points is strongly tied to the common view. Fourth, it might be objected that Reid's appeal to abilities is just an appeal to a *supplementary* way of discovering if someone has a concept; it is not a full *replacement* for the search for sensations. The first three qualifications reflect the fact that Reid's *main* concern was not to eliminate the "mental entity" analysis of concepts, but rather to attack the idealist theory explaining how such entities were produced. The arguments used to attack the theory of concept formation embody or presuppose the new analysis of "having a concept of x." They implicitly show the importance of the alternative but are not intended to emphasize a substitute theory so much as to show the weakness of an existing theory. The fourth objection overlooks Reid's main point, that in the case of primary qualities there are no sensations of the sort required by H1 and its corollary; for these cases it is a *replacement* for the search for sensations. The true qualification required here is that Reid does not propose his alternative as a new analysis for all concepts, but only for visible figure and primary qualities, that is, only for what we might call "theory bound" concepts. In this way, The Argument from the Blind Mathematician extends and completes the attack on the Ideal System begun in the Argument for No Special Sensations.

4. *The Geometry of Visibles and the Case for Realism*

The Argument from the Blind Mathematician contains most of the main ideas that are used in Reid's presentation of the geometry of visibles: the argument that one can apply a metric to visible space (based on the degree of difference in "position with regard to the eye") and can thus treat visible objects as subject to mathematical study; the relation between visible figures and their projections on a sphere; and the rationale for claiming visible space is two dimensional. *Reid's whole effort to prove that visibles are objects of mathematical study is just a special case of a general kind of problem he has to solve in order to attack the Ideal System and make his defense of realism.* Namely, he has to show that certain key concepts we have are bound up in intricate bodies of theory, such as primitive mechanics (concepts of primary qualities) or geometrical optics (visible figure). Far from Reid's discovery that visibles are models for a non-Euclidean geometry being totally divorced from *all* relevant scientific problems and practice, it becomes clear that a certain body of scientific problems and practice is unexpectedly "relevant." Reid's main ideas for the geometry of visibles grow directly out of 18th-century theory of vision and 18th-century theory of mind: they are not theoretical freaks totally divorced from scientific practice; they are not ideas which have fallen from the sky.

I have argued that Reid has some central metaphysical motives for attacking the theory of concept formation and the analysis of "having a concept" put forward by the idealists. The cognitive psychological mechanisms play a key role in making it seem plausible that concepts have to have corresponding sensations (H1), and so play an important part in the arguments that lead to skepticism or idealism. Reid is intent on developing a theory of mind compatible with common sense realism. The group of four main arguments dealing with figure and extension are attempts to clear out of the way the obstacle to such a theory, the dominant theory of concept formation, H1. But it would be a mistake to treat these arguments as attempts to "prove" that some version of realism is true. Rather, they really presuppose that there are "real" bodies having "real" properties, some which cause sensations. Reid shows that this materialist presupposition does *not* lead to idealism or skepticism *unless* we saddle ourselves with a false theory of concept formation and, perhaps, with a wrong analysis of what concepts are. One must see that Berkeley, especially in the *New Theory of Vision,* is the major enemy here.

Berkeley had argued that visible figure and extension are "in the mind." I have already noted his argument that figure and extension are "inseparable" from colors, which every-one agreed are not "without the mind."[42] Reid's reply, as I show in both the Argument from the Blind Mathematician and

Argument for the Independence of Color and Figure, is that visible figure and extension are indeed "separable" from color, for the blind man can perceive no color but can still have an adequate conception of visible figure and extension. That is, Reid argues that even if color is "in the mind," an assumption he rejects in the Argument from Common Knowledge, still Berkeley has not by that assumption proved that visible figure and extension are. On the other hand, Reid's Argument from the Blind Mathematician cannot be construed as a *proof* that visible figures are "real and external" to the eye or mind, even though Reid repeats this claim several times in the course of that Argument. For example, someone might argue that visible figure is a mathematical construction and shares the status of all mathematical objects. In this case, the realism-idealism debate will reemerge, but now with regard to the type of object the blind mathematician can know about: is a construction real or ideal? Further, by Reid's own descriptions, visible figure is no more "abstract," no less a mathematical construction, than real (tangible) figure. So, if the debate still infects visible figure, it will spread to real figure as well. If we read Reid's argument as an *ad hominem* reply to Berkeley's halfway house position in the *New Theory of Vision*—visual objects "in" but tangible objects "out" (cf. Chapter III)—then showing the connection in mathematical theory between tangible (real) and visible figure can have the effect of pulling everything "in" or pushing everything "out." Of course, Berkeley really wanted everything "in," so Reid cannot rest satisfied with this *ad hominem,* which, turned about, can be redirected against himself.

The arguments on figure and extension all have the function of refuting Berkeley's arguments for idealism, not the function of demonstrating the truth of realism. Nevertheless they still make a contribution to a pro-realist position. Reid's overall argument against the Ideal System is really quite sophisticated, as I show. He says that adherence to the ideal theory of mind leads to skeptical and idealist conclusions which run counter to common sense. Now, perhaps some common sense beliefs can be overruled as a

result of scientific or philosophical advance, especially when
the new scientific theories are based on firm arguments and
are widely accepted. But when so many such beliefs are
challenged at once, as in the case of the Ideal System, the
arguments leading to the skeptical and idealist conclusions
become suspect. Reid challenges those premises which act as
the major supports of the "ideal" theory of mind. Specifically,
the arguments on figure and extension are intended to
produce crucial counter examples to those premises. It is the
combination of these attacks on the foundations of the Ideal
System *plus* the heavy plausibility weighting given to common
sense that comprises Reid's case for realism.

Chapter V:

Reid's Nativism

1. *Reid's Nativism: Four applications*

In Chapter IV, I explain how Reid's interest in treating visible figure as an object of mathematical study grew out of his attack on the dominant 18th-century theory of concept formation. Reid argues that certain of our central concepts, especially the concepts of primary qualities, function as elements in a universally held theory of the basic properties of bodies. In this way, Reid hopes to show that we can possess and apply these concepts without having corresponding sensations, that is, independently of the mechanism of concept formation which is a central feature of the Ideal System. For example, a blind mathematician, who has never had visual sensations, can still learn the geometry of visibles, discriminate among the visible figures of real bodies, and therefore acquire and apply the concept of visible figure. The arguments Reid offers in his attacks on the Ideal System are part of his defense of realism. He wants to shatter the arguments offered for idealism by Berkeley, arguments Hume says cannot be answered. He wants to show that a scientific theory of the mind is compatible with realism. In these attacks, Reid is at his best.

But Reid does not stop with attacking the Ideal System and its theory of concept formation. He proposes an alternative, nativist theory intended to explain the origin of a variety of concepts and beliefs. I point out several times in previous chapters that Reid sometimes claims certain concepts, principles, and beliefs are given to us "by our constitution." In this chapter I show just what form Reid's nativism takes. In particular I discuss several main applications of Reid's Nativist theory: to explain certain visual phenomena, to explain how we form concepts of primary qualities, to shield us from the skeptic, and to serve as the basis for a philosophy of geometry and a more general theory of unrevisability.

Reid devotes almost a third of the *Inquiry* to showing that "some phenomena of the eye, and of vision, which have commonly [e.g., by Berkeley] been referred to custom, to anatomical or to mechanical causes . . . must be resolved into original powers and principles of the human mind."[1] In this task Reid often follows the lead of William Porterfield, a prominent 18th-century physician and researcher on the eye. I show in Chapter II, for example, that Porterfield attributes our seeing visual points as external to the eye to an "original and connate law."[2] Porterfield's suggestion in this case motivated Reid's feature (g) in his construction of the geometry of visibles (see Chapter I, Sect. 1).

The difference between Reid (and Porterfield) and Berkeley, in this debate on custom versus innate mechanism, is part of the more general attack on idealism. As part of his idealist stance, as I note in Chapter II, Berkeley thinks all sensory inputs have to be conscious. Consequently, the only learning mechanism he considers is one developed to handle conscious inputs. Reid thinks various inputs are not conscious. At least, he is sure that the only conscious inputs we have in certain cases, for example introspectible touch sensations, cannot explain how we form concepts of primary qualities (cf. Chapter IV, Sect. 3). To back up his central arguments on concept formation, Reid wants to show that non-conscious inputs play a wider role in learning than Berkeley allows. This explains his desire to eliminate "habit" and "custom," which depend on conscious inputs, wherever possible in the theory of vision.

Reid argues that "original powers and principles" must be invoked to account for our ability to maintain parallel motion of the eyes in attending to and in tracking objects,[3] to see the real, not the "inverted" position of objects,[4] and to see single with two eyes (the various phenomena of single and double vision).[5] For example, if the ability to maintain parallel motion of the eyes were acquired by habit, then one should expect infants to have serious difficulty directing both eyes in the same way. Since such distortions are not seen in children, it seems "to be extremely probable, that previous to custom, there is something in the constitution, some natural instinct, which directs us to move both eyes always the same way."[6] Actually, in this example, Reid attributes to "instinct" an ability which Porterfield says becomes necessary through habit:

> the uniform motion of our eyes is not at first necessary, but . . . the mind has imposed upon itself that Law, founded upon utility and advantage, that arises from this sort of motion, which motion does in time become so necessary that none of us are now able to move one eye towards any object but the other is likewise turned the same way.[7]

Reid says in contrast that only the fine eye adjustments are acquired through habit.[8] Most of the cases of "original powers and principles" picked out by Reid have their precedents in Porterfield and so should be seen as features of ongoing 18th-century problem solving in the theory of vision.

The nativist hypothesis is treated as a working hypothesis for these problems in mid-18th-century theory of vision. Reid's general procedure in using such an hypothesis is as follows. First he tries to find some testable or observable consequence of the counter-hypothesis that the ability is acquired and exercised as a result of reasoning or habit. The prediction about eye motion in infants is an example of such a consequence. Then, if existing learning theory as put forward by Berkeley and Hume can not account for the acquisition of the ability, Reid turns almost directly to his nativist hypothesis. He makes little effort to elaborate or modify 18th-century learning theory so that it might account for the ability in question.

Sometimes the point at which Reid stops in his effort to isolate "original principles" is determined by his rather conservative philosophy of science, which depends on a narrow interpretation of Newton's *regulae*.[9] Reid argues, for example, that a principle about corresponding points on the retina is the most general one he can find with which to explain seeing single with two eyes. This principle is then treated as a law of nature[10] and further speculation about the causes of our seeing single is ruled out, as a violation of Newton's *regulae* (cf. Chapter II, Sect. 1). Still, Reid does admit that we might find "more general" principles into which a given, apparently "original" principle could be resolved.[11] Thus, what might otherwise appear to be rather dogmatic in Reid's account—his all-to-quick retreat to a nativist claim—can, if viewed sympathetically, look like the work of a cautious scientist who is driven to nativism for fear of "speculating" beyond what is warranted by his data.

It is not of relevance to my discussion here to determine which of the visual abilities Reid thinks are given "by our constitution" are in fact learned, according to modern theory of vision. It would take me too far afield, for example, to discuss whether or not an "original" feature, such as "corresponding points on the retina," plays any role in our acquisition of the servo-mechanisms that adjust eye position. Of greater importance is showing just what is meant when Reid claims a feature, like his "corresponding points," is given to us "by our constitution." The point is that Reid seems to be claiming no more, at times, than that we must be constructed in certain rather specific ways, or else we could not acquire certain abilities. In other words, without certain built-in structural features of our "constitution," we could not make use of relevant sensory inputs and develop a particular ability. To use our previous example, without built-in "corresponding points," we would have no reference point by use of which we could produce distinct vision and learn to make fine eye adjustments. But, as we shall see, Reid goes far beyond the minimal claim that we are natively given certain structures, and instead he claims we are natively given concepts or beliefs.

Reid often advances his nativist hypothesis as a developmental one: "the faculties, by which . . . [an infant] perceives an external world . . . unfold themselves by degrees."[12] Some "original" powers are fully developed from birth; others may not be. Here, however, a problem arises. Reid never tells us how to distinguish *native* mental abilities or operations that develop an exposure to the senses from *acquired* mental abilities learned through habit or custom. This problem is somewhat complicated by the fact that our ability to acquire certain habits is itself given to us natively: "No part of the human constitution is more admirable than that whereby we acquire habits which are found useful without design or intention."[13] It is possible that the distinction Reid needs can be made in terms of the kind of input: acquired mental abilities, which rely on habit or custom, involve conscious inputs, whereas native mental abilities involve non-conscious inputs. But this is a rather complicated question which would take me far afield. To answer it I would have to elaborate the background theory of mind in considerable detail, as I suggest in Chapter II. Without that elaboration, it remains somewhat unclear just what the nativist claim means.

Reid uses a nativist hypothesis in his theory of concept formation as well as in his theory of vision. I show in Chapter IV how Reid rejects attempts to "derive" the concepts of primary qualities from touch sensations. Instead, he says that such concepts are *suggested* to us, in accordance with the "laws of our constitution," when we have certain touch impressions. I analyse Reid's nativism with regard to primary qualities into three claims:

   a) we develop clear and distinct conceptions of primary qualities;
   b) our conceptions of primary qualities are "suggested" to us when we have certain sensory experiences;
   c) what is "suggested" to us is a result of our having a particular constitution.

Included among the concepts of primary qualities are not only the concepts of mechanical qualities, like hardness, but also the concepts of geometrical qualities, like figure and extension. Together, these concepts are central to a

universally held, primitive theory of bodies, the elementary
mechanics discussed in the last chapter. Similarly, if these
three claims are combined with Reid's claim that all "first
principles,"[14] as well as the ability to see "necessary
relations,"[15] are given to us by our constitution, then the
whole framework for Reid's nativist philosophy of geometry
(to be discussed shortly) is revealed.

I discuss claim (a) in Chapter IV. Reid says,

> All mankind are *led by their constitution* to conclude
> hardness from this feeling . . . ⌊from⌋ the sensation we
> have by pressing a hard body . . . we conclude a
> quality of which we have a *clear and distinct* conception.[16]

It should be remembered that a concept is clear when our
definition of it contains only basic or primitive terms from
the universally held theory of bodies.[17] Minimally, Reid is
claiming we have a disposition to form clear and distinct
concepts of these qualities when we are exposed to the appropriate inputs. Maximally, Reid is claiming these clear and
distinct concepts are pre-programmed in our nature, as it
were, and need only the right input cues to bring them into
explicit play. It is somewhat unclear which of these maximal
or minimal claims Reid intends. In the case of secondary
qualities, we are natively given a disposition to form only
"unclear" and "indistinct" conceptions. For example, our
concept or "notion" of heat is, "the unknown cause of a certain known sensation." Reid states his nativist hypothesis in
this way: "by our constitution we conclude from . . . ⌊the
sensation of heat⌋ an obscure or occult quality, of which we
have only this relative conception, that it is something
adapted to raise in us the sensation of heat."[18]

The ambiguity in claim (a)—is Reid saying we simply
have a *disposition,* "by our constitution," to form clear and
distinct concepts of primary qualities, or is he saying we have
these *concepts* "by our constitution" and that they are just
brought into play (perhaps gradually) when we get the right
sensory inputs—is related to a more serious problem we
encounter in understanding claims (b) and (c). I show above in
my discussion of nativism in Reid's theory of vision that he

fails to provide a clear distinction between *natively* given abilities that *develop* on exposure to sensory inputs and *acquired* abilities that are *learned* as a result of sensory experience. This same problem, as we shall see, affects Reid's nativist account of the origins of primary quality concepts.

This problem lies buried in Reid's irksome word "suggestion." In Chapter IV I show that Reid often claims that our concepts of primary qualities are "suggested" either by sensations of touch or by material impressions on the organs of touch. *Suggestion* is a "power of the mind . . . to which we owe many of our simple notions which are neither impressions nor ideas, as well as many original principles of belief."[19] It is characteristic of "suggestion" that it involves "no comparing of ideas, no perception of agreements or disagreements,"[20] and no "reasonings" from premises.[21] Some "suggested" beliefs require that we have had certain experiences in the past—for example, a belief that a coach is passing "suggested" by a certain sound. In these cases Reid's "suggestion" is rather like Malebranche's "natural judgments."[22] But other "suggested" conceptions of primary qualities are "natural." Among them are the conceptions of primary qualities we receive from touch: "certain sensations of touch, by the constitution of our nature, suggest to us extension, solidity, and motion."[23] Reid's point in introducing these "natural" suggestions is to exclude the idea that we *learn* these conceptions of primary qualities by means of mental operations (which become habitual) involving introspectible inputs (sensations).

The problem, as in the case of the theory of vision, is that some "suggestions" do not arise instantly, upon exposure to the appropriate sensations or impressions. Some conceptions "suggested" to us by sensations do not exist in a developed form awaiting only certain sensations to occasion their emergence into consciousness. Rather, Reid leaves room for a developmental view of these constitutionally endowed conceptions:

> I do not mean to affirm, that the sensations of touch do
> from the very first suggest the same notions of body and

its qualities, which they do when we are grown up. Perhaps nature is frugal in this, as in her other operations . . . the faculties, by which it [the child in the womb] perceives an external world, by which it reflects on its own thoughts, and existence, and relation to other things, as well as its reasoning and moral faculties, unfold themselves by degrees.[24]

Let us look in some more detail at the problem underlying Reid's developmental nativism. Some beliefs and conceptions are a result of *learning through experience.* Other beliefs and conceptions, those we have "by our constitution," are a result of the *development* of our native faculties and powers through *exposure to sensory experience.* What is the difference between these processes of *learning* and *developing?*

Reid's implicit answer to this question, extracted from his practice, is not satisfying. Reid seems to take a given belief and ask whether it is at all plausible that we can arrive at it through the accepted 18th-century learning theory mechanisms. If he gets (or wants to get) a negative answer, then he concludes that the conception or belief must be given to us natively. For example, the (acquired) suggestion that a stagecoach is passing when we hear a certain sound is something Reid thinks can be explained within the framework of 18th-century learning theory. On the other hand, the clear and distinct conception and belief in a hard body suggested when we press a hard object is not explainable, on Reid's view, by 18th-century theory of concept formation or learning theory. Reid's implicit answer to the question, what distinguishes *learning* from natively *developing,* seems to come down to this: if a conception or belief cannot be explained by 18th-century theory of concept formation and learning theory, then it is not learned; but if it is not learned, then how else could we have gotten it, except as something which we developed "by our constitution"? The answer is no more satisfying than any half-hearted, "what else could it be?" argument.

Consider an example of one of Reid's "what else could it be?" arguments. A clear example begins with the thought experiment about touch sensations discussed in Chapter IV. We are asked to imagine a blind man who is deprived of *all* conceptions that play any role in the general theory of bodies and who is subjected to a variety of tactical sensations—pin pricks, varying pressure from blunt bodies, objects dragged across his skin, sensations from moving a limb. Reid argues the subject cannot "derive" any clear and distinct conception of primary qualities from those sensations. "Common sense" might lead him to form the *un*clear and *in*distinct conception, "unknown cause of this known sensation of a pin prick." But there is nothing introspectible in the sensation of the pin prick to lead him to a clear and distinct conception of, and belief in, the existence of a hard, figured body. "Having had formerly no notion of body or of extension, the prick of the pin can give him none."[25] Similarly, there is nothing introspectible in the sensation of a body dragged along his hand that should "convey the notion of space and motion, to one who had none before."[26]

In each of these examples, the first stage of Reid's "what else could it be?" argument consists of a "proof" that mechanisms allowed by 18th-century learning theory and theory of concept formation cannot yield the desired conception. Reid generalizes his argument for these instances to include the "first origins" of our notions of all primary qualities:

> Upon the whole, it appears, that our philosophers have imposed upon themselves, and upon us, in pretending to deduce from sensation the first origin of our notions of external existences, of space, motion, and extension, and all the primary qualities of body, that is, the qualities where of we have the most clear and distinct conception. These qualities do not at all tally with any system of the human faculties that hath been advanced.[27]

Reid backs up the first stage by arguing that we cannot come up with any obvious alternative to the existing 18th-century theories since introspection and memory will also not help us. "When we trace the operation of our minds as far back as memory and reflection can carry us, we find them already in possession of our imagination and belief, and quite familiar to the mind."[28]

But if the dominant theories do not account for these notions, and we cannot trace their history in any other obvious way, then how else can we account for them except by attributing them to our constitution? That is, Reid completes the "what else could it be?" argument:

> That our sensations of touch indicate something external, extended, figured, hard or soft, is not a deduction of reason, but a natural principle. The belief of it, and the very conception of it, are equally parts of our constitution. If we are deceived in it, we are deceived by him that made us, and there is no remedy.[29]

This conclusion, we should note, applies to both the "notion" and the "belief":

> The notion of hardness [for example] in bodies, as well as the belief of it, are got in a similar manner; being by an original principle of our nature, annexed to that sensation which we have when we feel a hard body.[30]

Reid's "what else could it be?" argument is applied to all "first principles," not just to the concept of primary qualities. As we shall see in a moment, Reid includes among his "first principles" many of the claims attacked by the skeptic—trustworthiness of the senses and memory, the uniformity of nature, the existence of minds[31]—as well as all mathematical axioms and the ability to recognize necessary relations and carry out deductions. Reid says that all such principles are parts of

> our constitution, no less then the power of thinking . . . How or when I got such first principles, upon which I build all my reasoning, I know not; for I had them before I can remember: but I am sure they are parts of my constitution, and that I cannot throw them off.[32]

In other words, no existing theory can explain how one arrives at the necessity of assenting to them, and there is no obvious alternative theory, "so" they must be parts of our constitution. What else could they be? How else could we get them?

It might be objected that there is an alternative interpretation of Reid's claims. Instead of taking Reid's remarks about "our constitution" to mean he is advancing a nativist position based on a "what else could it be?" argument, perhaps I should interpret Reid to be pleading ignorance about what mental mechanism or learning theory is appropriate. Perhaps he is simply insisting that *some* adequate theory will eventually be forthcoming and that all we can be sure of at this point is that we will have to know more about our constitution. This alternative interpretation might draw some support from Reid's materialist remark, "in the world of thought, the materials are all made by nature . . . the result of our constitution. The conception of extension, motion, and the other attributes of matter . . . must be the work of nature."[33] Similarly, Reid says that the connection between our having certain sensations and our acquiring conceptions and beliefs about external existences "is the effect of our constitution, and ought to be considered as an original principle of human nature, *till we find some more general principle into which it may be resolved."*[34] Perhaps Reid is saying that the principles he picks out as "original" may not seem like natively given principles once we have a better theory of concept formation. On the other hand, Reid's last remark is ambiguous: the "more general principle" might be yet another natively given principle, or it might be that new and better theory of concept formation.

The effort to save Reid from nativism is not likely to succeed. Reid refers to the "first principles" as original. Of course, he does allow for development of these "original" principles through exposure to sensations. Still, Reid seems to be committed to at least this claim: the human constitution is natively differentiated in certain rather specific ways, with the consequence that when we are given certain sensations or material impressions on sense organs, we form or are able to bring to consciousness certain concepts and beliefs automatically, "by the laws of our constitution."

If the effort to save Reid from this developmental nativism is serious, it must be claiming that Reid is seeking a very different *kind* of learning theory or theory of concept formation, some sophisticated improvement on 18th-century theories, perhaps. There seems to be little textual evidence to support the claim that Reid is looking for any such alternative. He never tries to elaborate one. In fact, such an alternative would seem to undermine what Reid hopes to get from his nativism, an explanation why certain conceptions and beliefs are inescapable and cannot be shaken. "By the constitution of our nature we are under a necessity of assenting to them."[35] That is, we cannot help but develop these notions and there is no way, short of altering our constitutions, to get rid of them. Any alternative to a nativist interpretation of Reid would have to provide for this degree of entrenchment.

What Reid desires from his nativism is not the claim that we have these notions, concepts, or beliefs fully formed at birth, but that we are so constituted that we inevitably and irrevocably develop them. That is, by our constitution, certain of our beliefs are unrevisable. It is this thrust of Reid's nativism, intended both to meet the skeptic head on and to replace his theory of concept formation, that is the basis for Reid's version of synthetic *a priori* propositions, as I show. To better reveal this motivation behind Reid's nativism, I will look at three main examples of how Reid tries to equip us from birth with protection against skepticism and idealism.

One cluster of related abilities and dispositions, "given to us by our constitution," permits us to "trace particular facts and observations to general rules,"[36] to "observe connections" between events,[37] and to search for the cause of things.[38] In other words, we are constructed in such a way that we function as 18th-century induction machines. Hume had tried to show that our knowledge of the world is built up through the exercise of habits and dispositions which we acquire upon being exposed to certain sensory inputs. Reid differs here from Hume in that he makes explicit what is often implicit in Hume, namely, that we *bring to experience* a "constitution" *natively* disposed to respond in certain ways to sensory inputs, ways which enable us to perceive order in our future experiences. Reid is not content with making explicit these natively given *abilities*. In addition he builds into "our constitution" the specific *belief* in the principle of the uniformity of nature. In this way he rather dogmatically "solves" Hume's puzzle about induction, that we have no way of justifying our belief that the future will resemble the past. By treating the principle of uniformity as a "first principle," part of our constitution, Reid is free to argue about it as he does about other principles given by our constitution: "If we are deceived in it, then we are deceived by him that made us, and there is no remedy."[39] I return shortly to other principles to which we are under a necessity to assent.[40]

In addition to defending induction against the skeptic, Reid also tries to defend our belief that our senses inform us about a real, external world. According to Reid, we are in general disposed to attend to things signified by signs (where a sign might be a visible figure, for example) rather than to the signs themselves.[41] Interestingly enough, the idea to take this particular disposition as native arose in the theory of vision. Porterfield made exactly this claim: ". . . tho' all our sensations are passions or perceptions produced in the mind itself, yet the mind never considers them as such, but, by an irresistible law of nature, it is always made to refer them to something external."[42] Thus a claim which Reid uses as a weapon against the skeptic has its origin in problem solving activity in the theory of vision and not just in a debate between two epistemological opponents. Once again, philosophic theory has specific ties to scientific practice.[43]

Accompanying our disposition to attend to the things signified by (sensory) signs is a natively given *conception* of external, existing things and events, as well as a *belief* in their externality and existence. That is, we are so constructed that when our senses present us with certain signs, there arise in us conceptions and beliefs about a real world.[44]

A third set of anti-skeptical dispositions serves to provide *prima facie* confidence in the testimony of our senses and memories, and in the testimony of others. Reid anticipates some contemporary anti-skeptical arguments when he claims that we are disposed to trust the testimony of our senses. But not only do we trust our senses, we also are disposed to believe the testimony of memory. Memories, by the laws of our constitution, give rise to the conception of, and belief in, externally existing objects and events of the past. "Upon the strictest attention, memory appears to me to have things that are past, and not present ideas, for its object."[45] Finally, not only are we disposed by our constitution to trust our own senses and memories; we are also natively disposed to speak the truth and to confide in the veracity of others.[46] (Incidentally, Reid here appears to anticipate Wittgenstein's claim that some such disposition is a precondition for the possibility of instruction of any kind).

These three groups of anti-skeptical abilities, dispositions, and beliefs are among those which Reid groups together as "common sense." Common sense puts us under a necessity to form certain conceptions and hold certain beliefs. It provides us with fixed points in our theories. Since these inescapable, unrevisable beliefs include many which are not traditionally classified as *a priori*, Reid is giving us a rather broad theory of unrevisable beliefs. Before I discuss the general statement of this theory of unrevisability and some problems that arise from it, I want briefly to look at a special application of it. I want to show how Reid's nativism provides the basis for his philosophy of geometry. I believe that my discussion of how we form our notions of primary qualities helps show how Reid thinks we form our notions of mathematical points, lines, angles, and figures.

Reid's nativist philosophy of geometry contains at least three main claims:

(1) The notions which we have of mathematical points, lines, angles, and figures are determined by our constitutions.[47]
(2) We can see the necessary relations holding between points, lines, angles, and figures because of a natively endowed ability.[48]

(3) We can "form geometrical conclusions, built upon
self-evident principles."[49]

Points (2) and (3) require little discussion. As I show, Reid
argues that all reasoning, including mathematical reasoning,
will be from "first principles" which are parts of our
constitution. "By the constitution of our nature, we are under
a necessity of assenting to them."[50] How can we pick out this
class of mathematical principles? The only criterion for
membership seems to be whether or not we must assent to
them. Reid gives us no other way of picking them out nor of
determining how large a class it is.

In addition to equipping us natively with an
indeterminate class of first principles, Reid also gives us the
ability to see the necessary relations between, say, points,
lines, angles, and figures. He does not seem to think that we
natively possess a conception and belief in each such relation,
but only that we are capable of detecting all such relations.

What is of importance here, however, is Reid's account
of how we come to have notions of mathematical points, lines,
angles and figures. It parallels exactly his account of how we
come to form concepts of primary qualities. Reid's only
discussion of this aspect of his nativism in the *Inquiry* occurs
when he explains how the Idomenian, his imaginary touchless
being, would develop a geometry, the non-Euclidean
geometry of visibles. The main point Reid makes is that the
Idomenian is constitutionally unequipped to have any
"notion" of a third dimension. Because he is equipped only
with vision, "by his constitution" he can have only two
dimensions "suggested" to him through sensory experience.[51]
Consequently, Reid argues, his notions of points, lines,
angles, and figures will be "less determined" than ours. "In the
notion of a point, we exclude length, breadth, and thickness;
he excludes length, and breadth, but cannot either exclude or
include thickness, because he hath no conception of it."[52]
Similarly, in Reid's two-dimensional visual space, a right line
can "return to itself": "its being straight to the eye, implies
only straightness in one dimension."[53] Further, as I note, Reid

can specify a metric, taking the "infinite" right line as a unit: "In like manner, the common and natural measure of length, is an infinite right line, which, as hath been before observed, returns to itself, and hath no limits, but bears a finite *ratio* to every other line."[54]

Reid's account can be summed up as a threefold claim. One, visual space is two-dimensional and non-Euclidean. Two, our visual experience is experience of a two-dimensional, non-Euclidean space. Three, "by our constitution," if we are restricted to vision alone, we can form mathematical notions appropriate only to a two-dimensional, non-Euclidean geometry. The first claim makes clear Reid's realism. I return to all three claims in the next section.[55]

The central point in Reid's discussion is his contention that the Idomenian's constitution determines just which geometry he will develop. Since he can develop only a certain set of mathematical notions, he is equipped to develop only a two-dimensional, non-Euclidean geometry. Accordingly, there must be a parallel restriction for humans. We are equipped "by our constitution" to develop a three-dimensional, Euclidean geometry of tangible space. Consequently, we are under necessity, by our constitution, to treat tangible space as three-dimensional and Euclidean. Since Reid identifies tangible and real space, as I note in Chapter I, Sect. 2, we are under necessity, by our constitution to treat real space as three-dimensional and Euclidean. For example, the Idomenian "could have no notion of a third dimension, any more than we can have of a fourth."[56] All of our notions of points, lines, angles, figures, and planes will be "determined" in three dimensions by our constitution, just as the Idomenians' are determined in two dimensions.

Of course, by our constitution we can develop both geometries, one for real (tangible) space, the other for visible space, provided that we can train ourselves to attend to the visibles. Thus sensations or material impressions on our sense organs are what "suggest" the basic mathematical notions. *But they can suggest only those notions which we are natively equipped and disposed to develop.* Since these notions are in this sense given to us by our constitution, as are our first principles and our ability to see mathematical relations, then geometrical propositions will be those which we are led to develop and forced to assent to "by our constitution." They will not be revisable.

2. *Reid's Theory of Unrevisability*

In the previous section, I discuss the origins of Reid's nativism in 18th-century theory of vision (Porterfield), its epistemological function in shielding us from the skeptic, and its function as an alternative theory of concept formation to that advanced in the Ideal System. Finally, I explain how the nativist theory of concept formation serves as a basis for Reid's philosophy of geometry. That nativist philosophy of geometry has as its key feature the claim that sensory experience elicits from us ("suggests") the formation of certain mathematical concepts or notions and beliefs which the laws of our constitution determine us to develop. These concepts and beliefs are "parts of our constitution" and "we are under a necessity of assenting to them."[57] That is, it is not possible for us to revise them.

Reid's philosophy of geometry, however, is only part of a broader theory of unrevisable conceptions and beliefs. I mention above all the anti-skeptical and anti-idealist beliefs which, along with first principles of mathematics, are the core of "common sense." In other words, Reid includes many beliefs which are not traditionally included in the category of the *a priori*, let alone those which are not thought to be analytical or "relations of ideas." He includes many beliefs which are obviously learned.

But the important assumption underlying all of Reid's theory is the claim that anything which is "part of our constitution" is unrevisable. In what sense are these beliefs unrevisable? For one thing, as I have shown, Reid says we are under a necessity to assent to them. We cannot come to believe they are false. In fact, we are constructed so that it is impossible for us to believe that they are false. Presumably, as

a result of the way we are designed, neither arguments nor
sensory experience can produce in us a belief in the falsity of
these natively determined beliefs. "[R]eason can neither make
nor destroy them . . . I am sure they are parts of my
constitution, and that I cannot throw them off."[58]

More importantly, Reid thinks it is impossible for us to
do without these natively given concepts and beliefs. He offers
two arguments for this claim. First, we can carry out no
reasonings without using these principles as starting points. As
Reid puts it, reason cannot "do anything without them."[59]
This point is true not only in mathematics ("A mathematician
cannot prove the truth of his axioms, nor can he prove
anything, unless he takes them for granted"), but also in
history ("it is taken for granted that the memory and senses
may be trusted") and in science ("it is taken for granted that
the course of nature is steady and uniform").[60]

But Reid's second argument to show we cannot do
without the beliefs we have by our constitution is more
important. Reid says we cannot *act* on beliefs that are
contrary to common sense. In pushing this argument Reid
seems to be relying on the more general principle that we test
our beliefs through action, through practice. The problem
with skeptical beliefs is that they cannot be acted on in
practice:

> When a man suffers himself to be reasoned out of the
> principle of common sense, by metaphysical arguments,
> we may call this *metaphysical lunancy;* which differs
> from the other species of distemper in this, that it is not
> continued, but intermittent; it is apt to seize the patient in
> solitary and speculative moments; but when he enters
> into society, Common Sense recovers her authority.[61]

A real weakness of Reid's position is that the very point
he makes in opposition to the skeptic—that skeptical beliefs
cannot be put into practice and are overruled by practice—is
a point which raises a serious question about his own theory of
unrevisability. If practice is the test of beliefs, then what is
Reid's argument that practice can never force us to revise

conceptions and beliefs we have "by our constitution"? Reid seems to believe that "by our constitution" we are restricted *both* to having certain *fixed points in our theories* about the world and to having *only that experience or practice compatible* with those fixed points.

An important point that Reid makes in another context seems to be in part responsible for Reid's restricting our experience in this way. Reid is critical of the idea, central to the Ideal System, that our perceptions are really images or like images. In contrast, he argues that "every operation of the senses, in its very nature, implies judgment or belief, as well as simple apprehension." His arguments on this point are often taken as an anticipation of the Gestaltists:

> [W] hen I feel the pain of the gout in my toe, I have not only a notion of pain, but a belief of its existence, and a belief of some disorder in my toe which occasions it; and this belief is not produced by comparing ideas, and perceiving their agreements and disagreements; it is included in the very nature of the sensation.[62]

The problem arises for Reid when the fixed beliefs we have by our constitution are conjoined with our perception and so serve as restrictions on what possible experiences we may have. These fixed beliefs seem to introduce a damaging constraint on an important area of practice, namely, a constraint on the ideas we can get from perception.

Consider an example of how such a fixed point might operate. Reid asks us to imagine what the geometry and physics of the touchless Idomenians might be like. I have already suggested that they will have only the two-dimensional, non-Euclidean geometry of visibles. Reid also argues that they will firmly believe that two bodies may occupy the same place at the same time:

> every Idomenian firmly believes, that two or more bodies may exist in the same place. For this they have the testimony of sense, and they can no more doubt of it, than they can doubt whether they have any perception at

> all. They often see two bodies meet, and coincide in the
> same place, and separate again, without having
> undergone any change in their sensible qualities by this
> penetration. When two bodies meet, and occupy the
> same place, commonly one only appears in that place,
> and the other disappears.[63]

It is important to remember that, "by their constitution," their
sensory experience can lead them to develop a conception of
only two dimensions. They "could have no notion of a third
dimension, any more than we can have of a fourth."[64]
Presumably, since we are determined, by our constitution, to
have a notion of only three dimensions, and all "testimony of
sense" confirms our belief that no two bodies can occupy the
same three-dimensional place at the same time, there is no way
for our perceptual practice to disconfirm our belief.

But now a skeptical problem arises. Cannot there be
some being with a different constitution whose theories show
what is wrong with our fixed beliefs, just as our theories show
what is wrong with the Idomenians"?[65] That is, by analogy to
the Idomenians, we may have constitutions which permit us to
develop only certain beliefs, beliefs which are "confirmed by
the testimony of sense," but which are systematically false as
are the beliefs of the Idomenians.

Reid is here driven to the verge of skepticism because he
shares with the empiricists a truncated notion of practice.
That is, he seems to think that the only practice relevant to the
confirmation and formation of our beliefs is perceptual
experience, primarily visual and tactual perception. Reid
complains that proponents of the Ideal System are not able to
explain how certain conceptions and beliefs can arise given
their notion of sensory experience. In response, Reid builds
those conceptions and beliefs into us natively, and, as was just
noted, into our perceptual experience. For example, Reid
thinks we have three-dimensional Euclidean tactual
perceptions and two-dimensional non-Euclidean visual
perceptions. Thus, Reid still thinks about the practice relevant
to our developing and using either geometry entirely within

the rather narrow limits set by his enemies, the empiricist proponents of the Ideal System.

Reid is making at least two important mistakes here. First, visual and tactual perception are themselves limited in a rather dogmatic way when Reid insists that perception can not disconfirm certain natively given beliefs. For example, he thinks the touchless Idomenians can never perceive one object disappearing behind another. We can imagine, however, that a freak or mutant Idomenian may emerge who can develop a concept of a third dimension and who can *perceive* one object disappearing behind another rather than just penetrating it. In other words, Reid's nativism leads him to restrict unnecessarily what is available to us even in perception.

Second, visual and tactual perception are not all there is to practice. Both Idomenians and humans develop concepts and beliefs based on a much wider notion of practice than visual or tactual perception alone. Reid offers no argument to show that since we have only Euclidean tactual experience, then we cannot develop alternative geometries applicable to tangible (real) space. In fact, Reid's blind mathematician develops the geometry of visibles at a level of abstraction considerably removed from the truncated notion of practice—that is, perception—which is generally assumed to be the whole story by both Reid and his opponents. When we restrict the practice relevant to belief testing and development just to perception, then both subsequent theory and practice suffer. A dogmatic approach to practice, in which only certain forms of practice are relevant, seems to be as damaging to the subsequent development of theory and practice as a dogmatic approach to theory, in which certain beliefs are held unrevisable.

Reid's only defense against the skeptical outcome of his own nativism—namely, that our constitutions might lead us to systematically false beliefs—is his belief that God would not deceive us. "If we are deceived . . . , we are deceived by him that made us, and there is no remedy."[66] Similarly, "[c]ommon sense and reason have both one author; that almighty Author, in all whose other works we observe a consistency, uniformity, and beauty, which charm and delight the understanding: there must therefore be some order and consistency in the human faculties."[67]

In his appeal to God—rather than to practice—to guarantee the truth of his realism, Reid diverges sharply from a full-fledged materialist epistemology. He seems willing to use the criterion of compatibility with practice to *reject skeptical beliefs*; in this appeal to practice he agrees with the materialists. But he does not rely on compatibility with practice as the appropriate test and justification *for realism*. A consistent materialist epistemology, as put forward by Marx, Engels or Lenin, and which was already being hinted at by 18th-century French contemporaries of Reid, would acknowledge compatibility with practice as the sole test for realism.

Rather than comment at this point on Reid's piety (cf. next section), I restrict myself to an important point that emerges even in his appeal to God. Reid maintains his realist stance; he tries not to slip into idealism, even if he does slip into dogmatism. God is guaranteeing our *knowledge* of the real world. It is not our constitution that *makes* the unrevisable propositions necessarily *true*. Rather, our constitution is designed by God to *reveal the truth*.

Perhaps this contrast can be illuminated by a brief comparison of Reid with Kant. What is the difference between Reid's claim, that certain beliefs we have "by our constitution" must be assented to and are guaranteed true by God's benevolence, and Kant's claim, that certain judgments are necessarily true because, say, they reflect the *a priori* "form of our intuition"? At first it might seem as if there really is no difference. Reid seems to be saying that we bring certain concepts and beliefs *to experience* "by our constitution," so of course we have the "testimony of sense" to confirm these beliefs. But it is really very far from Reid's view that our minds are instrumental in constructing the world. Reid never thinks that we *impose* a structure on experience, so that the world comes "necessarily" to have those features we put into it. To be sure, there is always Kant's disclaimer that we construct only the phenomenal world, and not the noumenal world. But this disclaimer still leaves Kant a quasi-idealist making concessions to idealism that Reid fights tooth and nail. Reid could never accept the distinction between phenomenal and noumenal worlds. Reid saves his realism only by appeal to dogmatism. Without God, Reid's nativism, with its unrevisable beliefs, might in fact push him into the very idealism and skepticism it was intended to save him from.

On the other hand, Reid does share some common ground with Kant. For example, it is not an empirical question, to be settled by experiment, what the geometry of space is. That is, Reid shares all the failings of Kant's philosophy of mathematics. Still, there is a difference even here. For Kant, the space we live in is Euclidean *because* the *a priori* form of our intuition determines its mathematical structure. For Reid, we know "by our constitution," which does not deceive us, that real space (tangible space) *is* Euclidean. Our constitution reveals the structure of space; it does not establish it.

3. *The Influence of Reid's Defense of Realism*

British Empiricism, including its theory of mind, the Ideal System, was ushered into prominence under the shelter of Locke's attack on nativism or innate ideas. Reid's critique of the Ideal System shows that it lacks an adequate theory of concept formation, especially with regard to the concepts of primary qualities, and therefore exposes a serious gap in its theory of mind. But instead of searching for a more sophisticated learning theory to explain the origins of these central concepts, Reid retreats under the umbrella of nativism. As I show, his retreat is rather unsatisfying: whatever we cannot explain the origins of in terms of 18th-century learning theory, we must have had from birth. Empiricism rose with an attack on innate ideas, and Reid expects to see it fall with a defense of them. I have already remarked how Reid justifies natively given "common sense" beliefs through a dogmatic appeal to God as a nondeceiver.

Reid's dogmatic defense of realism continued to have great influence in Scotland and America. Reid provided the philosophical background for a major effort to reconcile religion with the new advances in science. Reid's own background as a Moderate Clergyman may have had something to do with his motivation in fending off skeptical attacks at the same time he defended the utility of new science. The Moderates sought to reconcile religion and science and helped to avoid the enmity that existed in France between the philosophers and the theologians.[68] Reid's use of his realism, and the uses to which it was put by his followers, distinguishes him from the 18th-century French materialists, like Diderot and D'Alembert, who defended the new science at the expense of theology.

Reid's earlier epistemological views were developed in his later works, the *Essays on the Intellectual Powers of the Mind* (1785), and, applied to moral philosophy, with Hume once again as his chief opponent, in his *Essays on the Active Powers of the Human Mind* (1788). Both his epistemological and moral views were popularized in the works of James Beattie (1735-1803) and Dugald Stewart (1753-1828) and several others who collectively became known as the Scottish School of Common Sense. Even some of Reid's critics, like Thomas Brown (1778-1820) and William Hamilton (1778-1856) were considerably influenced by Reid.

Reid's influence abroad was also extensive. In France, Reid's ideas were used by Pierre Royer-Collard and Victor Cousin to attack the Lockean theory of mind. In Germany, Reid was remembered more for his dogmatic sins than his critical virtues. Kant, in his *Prolegomena to any Future Metaphysics,* lumped Reid with his even more dogmatic followers, Beattie and James Oswald, and charged them all with having "missed the point" of Hume's discussion of causation.

Reid's influence lasted longest, however, in the United States. John Witherspoon, president of The College of New

Jersey (later called Princeton) in the late 18th century, is perhaps the first to have introduced Reid's philosophical realism into America. His interest in realism came from wanting to answer the version of moral skepticism that derived from Hume through Lord Kames: if man cannot know the external world, and is therefore unable to change it, then he cannot be morally accountable for his actions.[69] If, as Reid showed, man's senses can be trusted within limits, then he is to that extent morally accountable. Witherspoon was intent on reconciling a "pious education" with the Enlightenment interest in science, therefore showing that a scientific theory of the mind need not lead to impiety was essential.[70]

Samuel Stanhope Smith, who also played an important role in administering The College of New Jersey after 1779, also saw in Reid the philosophical basis for reconciling religion and science. For example, Smith found Reid invaluable in avoiding the dual dangers of materialism and idealism, and the atheism that invariably followed from materialism.[71] Similarly, Smith drew on Reid in his discussion of scientific method, especially concerning the reliability of the senses.[72] The belief that it is possible to make scientific generalizations based on observation of human phenomena, which Smith shared with Reid and his followers, was a cornerstone in Smith's proposals for educational reform. Similarly, Reid was of considerable influence on Benjamin Rush and James McCosh who continued to use Reid's realism well into the 19th century as a way of reconciling science and "pious education."[73]

Reid's influence in America died late in the 19th century, somewhat earlier in England and Europe. Perhaps the rise of pragmatism, absolute idealism and materialism rendered Reid's particular defense of realism less effective or relevant. At any rate, in the 20th century Reid has primarily been remembered for his dogmatism. More recently, some attention has been given to Reid's views on the origins of language, which are found more in his later works than in the *Inquiry,* and to his view that there is a *prima facie* warrant for trusting the senses. But on the whole, the rather conservative and dogmatic uses to which Reid's ideas were put in the late 18th and early 19th centuries seem to have kept Reid from contemporary view. This is especially true in light of the popularity the 18th-century empiricists have enjoyed following the efforts of 20th-century positivists to revive them.

More recently, interest in Reid has again increased. New editions of his long-out-of-print major works are now available. But whatever turn Reid's new historical fortunes take, I believe I show that his defense of realism against Berkeley and Hume is a rich and profound critique, one that deserves far more attention than it has received.

I also show, I believe, that there is a special interest to Reid's defense of realism, an interest that goes far beyond the merits of his critique of the Ideal System. When combined with the 17th and 18th-century theory of vision and 18th-century theory of mind— the distance perception problem and the theses about "heterogeneity" and "natural signs" in particular—Reid's defense of realism in the *Inquiry* acts as a birthright for his discovery of a non-Euclidean geometry. Without this birthright the geometry of visibles is a theoretical scandal, born without benefit of any marriage between theory and practice. With its humble birthright uncovered, it is easier to see why the discovery of the geometry never rose to any great station in intellectual life. The importance and fruitfulness of scientific discoveries, if this case study proves anything, are often as much the products of scientific practice as the discoveries themselves. Reid himself treats the geometry of visibles as but an elaboration of a minor point about the heterogeneity of tactual and visual space and it plays only a supplementary role in his arsenal of arguments against 18th-century theory of concept formation. With such humble beginnings, it should not surprise us that the geometry has remained unnoticed for two hundred years. Far more surprising is the fact that Reid, working completely outside the mathematical community, manages to pull together the elements of his discovery from the philosophical and scientific tradition in which he works. I show, I believe, that even if this development is surprising, it is still explainable without our abandoning our belief in the intimate relation between theory and practice.

Afterword

Stepping into the world (even the nonfictional world) of the same book twice, including one's own book, may be as impossible as stepping into the same river twice. The author, like the reader, returns with an altered mind. In my case, the alterations are the result of my whole professional career, spent largely on other philosophical issues. That I would not now write the book as I then did must be weighed against the fact that I could not now write the book the same way. Nevertheless, that I would not now write it as I then did does not mean that I wish I had not so written it. Still, I do here want to point out some things I now think erroneous or misleading, at least in emphasis. I am grateful that Stanford University Press is giving me the chance to do so and, more important, is making the book available to students and scholars who have had so much trouble finding it in recent years.

The Geometry of Visibles

The central question that prompted me to write the book was this: how was Reid, who was not involved in contemporary work on the parallels postulate, led to discover a non-Euclidean geometry? My interest in Reid thus grew out of my graduate training in the philosophy of science and specifically out of my curiosity about the relationship between theoretical change and scientific practice. By showing that Reid's discovery was rooted in a rich tradition of scientific and philosophical work on the theory of vision and the theory of concept formation, I hoped to provide it with a birthright. At the same time, I hoped to explain why the discovery was not noticed for what it was.

I have come to believe that the question that motivated me is problematic in two ways. First, though it led me to investigate central themes in the *Inquiry,* themes which shape much of Reid's later philosophy as well, it also led me to cut off discussion of Reid's later development of these ideas in the *Essays.* I was able to answer the question to my satisfaction without leaving the confines of the *Inquiry.* As a result of pursuing material only as far as the motivating question led me, I thus fell short of writing a comprehensive book on all of Reid's philosophy. This restriction in the focus of the book clearly frustrated some reviewers,[1] but it is not a limitation I can rectify without writing a new book.

I can, however, rectify the second problem with my motivating question, namely that it is premised on a false assumption. In fact, contrary to my earlier belief (see p. 3 n. 2 above), Reid was familiar with some important eighteenth-century work on the parallels postulate. David Norton remarks,

> For Daniels to make these claims [that Reid was unfamiliar with contemporary work in geometry, including that of Saccheri] he must have limited his investigation to Reid's published works, ignoring even his biography. The Birkwood papers [deposited in the Library of King's College, Aberdeen] clearly indicate Reid's continuing concern with geometry, and specifically with the parallel postulate, and give ample evidence of his life-long concern with the body of mathematical practice. He was related by marriage to the mathematical Gregory family, who almost surely knew of his interest and competence in mathematics, and who would have been for him a ready source of information on the development of eighteenth-century mathematics.[2]

Norton is certainly right that I was unaware of the Birkwood papers and the light they throw on Reid's work on geometry. (These manuscripts were not available to scholars in the period I worked on the book.) I had, however, noted that a biography of Reid referred to a lecture on geometry Reid gave in 1761–62. These biographical allusions to his interest in mathematics were not specific enough to warrant any view other than the (mistaken) one that underlay my question.

Fortunately, later in the 1970's, Norton's student Susan

Weldon was able to examine these manuscripts carefully. In the appendix to her dissertation on Reid's theory of vision, she cites several unpublished letters in which Reid discusses Saccheri's work and comments on his own attempts to settle the status of Euclid's fifth postulate.[3] She notes that Reid in general agrees with Saccheri's (unsuccessful) refutation of the obtuse angle hypothesis and that he claims to have developed a similar argument. She remarks that this agreement between Saccheri and Reid might seem surprising, since Reid also believed that the fifth postulate does not follow from Euclid's axioms. But, she remarks, "Reid notes that Saccheri has assumed additional axioms and presumably Reid finds them acceptable."[4] Weldon notes that Reid's agreement with Saccheri is not complete: Reid does not approve of Saccheri's "reasonings about infinitesimals which Reid finds suspect." Instead, he suggests an alternative strategy for showing that the obtuse angle hypothesis is false.[5]

Contrary to my claims in Chapter I, then, Reid clearly was aware of some important eighteenth-century work on the parallels postulate. It is less clear, however, what the implications of this new information are. Reid's introduction of the 'geometry of visibles' in the *Inquiry* makes no reference to the ongoing work on the fifth postulate—which is what made his discovery puzzling in the way indicated by my motivating question. The setting for his discovery is still the one I describe—the new geometry is introduced to resolve a dispute between Reid and Berkeley about the "heterogeneity" of objects of vision and touch.

Still, Reid's views about Saccheri's work may make it seem less likely that he viewed his non-Euclidean geometry of visibles as an alternative to the "common" or Euclidean geometry. Weldon argues for such a conclusion. She notes that in his other comments on geometry, especially in the *Essays,* Reid seemed to think the parallels postulate was a necessary truth—even if it did not follow strictly from Euclid's first four axioms. Weldon draws the inference that Reid "cannot regard visible geometry as conflicting with Euclid's."[6]

My claim, however, is not that Reid thought his geometry was an alternative to Euclidean geometry for the three-dimensional space we live in. Rather, he believed it was an alternative, consistent geometry, even if it was only true of visible space (see p. 13 above). Indeed, Reid thought both geometries are "true" since each is tied *a priori,* that is, "by our constitution," to a special interpretation, in one case to visible space, in the other to tangible space. I tried to accommodate Reid's view that the parallels postulate is a necessary truth for the (tangible) space we live in by appealing to this nativist view (see Chapter V and for the reasons I offer in the book. Nevertheless, he did think that the geometry is a fully consistent alternative to Euclidean ge-Euclidean geometry, including its implications for our account of necessary truths, had he presented the geometry of visibles as a full-blown alternative to Euclidean geometry, he did not do so, and for the reasons I offer in the book. Nevertheless he did think that the geometry is a fully consistent alternative to Euclidean geometry, if only for two-dimensional visual space. (I might note that my central claims about Reid's discovery seem to have been accepted by most reviewers.)[7]

Throughout the book, I argue that the geometry of visibles is best understood as part of Reid's attack on the Ideal System and his defense of realism. I am not completely happy, however, with the account that emerges of what it is to see a visible object or a point in visible space. I end up claiming that Reid is in a predicament: "When we see a visible point, we are seeing an equivalence class of real points," that is, points in tangible space (see p. 19). This account makes visible points seem to be rather peculiar objects. We cannot, however, simply pick out an obvious set of real points—e.g., the projection of the boundary points of an object onto the retina or onto an arbitrary sphere with the Eye at the center—because any such set of real (tangible) points will presumably have a Euclidean geometry. So I settled for our seeing equivalence classes of real points, which is not a happy solution.

Others have since struggled with the same problem. David Norton suggests that we construe these non-Euclidean visible objects as "appearances" that stand as signs—natural or acquired—for real and Euclidean things.[8] Norton's "appearances" are not, however, sensations, in contrast to the treatment of the problem he ascribes to Timothy Duggan.[9] Weldon criticizes my account, claiming it results in our perceiving an "ideal" rather than a real object, and argues that visible space is the space of "positions with regard to the eye," which involves "actual relationships in real space."[10] This space offers a partial specification of location in real space. But, because of the transitivity of identity, if the points in this space are contained within real (tangible) space and are identical to real points, then their geometry would presumably be Euclidean geometry, contrary to hypothesis.

Weldon is drawn to her account by a passage she cites from the *Essays:*

> When I use the names of tangible and visible space, I do not mean to adopt Bishop Berkeley's opinion, so far as to think that they are really different things, and altogether unlike. I take them to be different conceptions of the same thing: the one very partial, and the other more complete; but both distinct and just as far as they reach. . . . Our sight alone, unaided by touch, gives a very partial notion of space, but yet a distinct one. When it is considered according to this partial notion, I call it visible space. The sense of touch gives a much more complete notion of space; and when it is considered according to this notion, I call it tangible space. (*Essays,* p. 325)[11]

This talk about "conceptions of the same thing" may be Reid's considered view in his later work, but it involves a rather different way of resolving his dispute with Berkeley about the heterogeneity of visible and tangible space from the view that emerges in the *Inquiry.* I still believe Reid agrees with Berkeley in his early work that they are heterogeneous spaces having distinct geometries. Nevertheless, my unease with my own interpretation of Reid makes me conclude that this dispute with Weldon is best viewed as not settled.

I might note that I have in general refrained from comparing early and late Reid, for the reason mentioned earlier; my motivating question was fully answered without examining the later work. But I cannot refrain from dissenting from John Immerwahr's view that Reid shifted from being an "indirect" realist to being a

"direct" realist.[12] The difference, according to Immerwahr, is
that in indirect realism, found in the *Inquiry,* physical impressions produce sensations which then "suggest" conceptions and
beliefs, whereas in direct realism, found in the *Essays,* physical
impressions cause "the awareness of the external object directly,
without the necessary intervention of the sensation."[13] Though
there are many places in the *Inquiry* where Reid gives sensations
this causal role, he also provides all the argument needed to show
that, in important cases, sensations can be bypassed, yielding a
version of direct realism. My arguments in Chapter III should be
read as urging this view.

Reid's Nativism

Especially in the *Inquiry,* as I suggest in Chapter V, but also
in both *Essays,* Reid often claims that we have certain perceptual
and cognitive abilities, concepts, and beliefs as a consequence of
the design or structure of our constitution.[14] The variety of such
abilities, concepts, and beliefs that we have "by our constitution"
is impressive. Various visual abilities, like maintaining uniform,
parallel motion of the eyes when attending to and tracking visual
objects; seeing the real, not the retinal ("inverted"), position of
objects; seeing single with two eyes; and seeing visual objects
as occupying a position in external visual space are all explained
by reference to original "laws of our constitution." The acquisition of clear and distinct concepts of primary qualities is explained by reference to the natural workings of our constitution
when we are exposed to the appropriate experiences. And, what
has often received the most attention, we are led by our constitution to form the unshakeable belief in the uniformity of nature,
the externality of the world revealed to us by our senses, the existence of a mind as the subject of our experiences, the first principles of logic and mathematics and morals. By our constitution,
then, we are led to form and "are under a necessity to assent
to" many of the beliefs directly attacked by eighteenth-century
skepticism.

As a defense against the skeptic, however, simply packing

our constitution with the disposition to develop and assent to first principles which the skeptic challenges is not a happy strategy— at least not if that is all that is done. After all, the fact that a belief is given to us by our constitution is not by itself a guarantee of its truth or a proof that it needs no further justification. Our constitution, the skeptic will insist, may be so (mis-)designed that we are systematically deceived. In that case, as Reid remarks, "We are deceived by Him that made us, and there is no remedy." [15]

In fact, as I point out in Chapter V, Reid even provides us with a model of such congenital deception when he tells us about the physics and geometry of his sighted but touch-blind beings, the Idomenians. These ancestors of Edwin Abbott's Flatlanders would be unable to conceive of three-dimensional space, since, on Reid's view, visual space is only two-dimensional and the concept of three-dimensionality can derive only from the sense of touch. As I suggest in Chapter V, the non-Euclidean geometry of visibles will be synthetic *a priori* for the Idomenians, anticipating Kant's philosophy of geometry. Corresponding distortions in the Idomenians' physics would result, for they would believe that two or more bodies may exist in the same place. Their experience, rooted in and limited by their defective constitution, does not allow them to conceive of one body passing behind another in visible space. The skeptic might hasten to remind us that we may suffer from similar congenital conceptual deformities.

In Chapter V, I claimed that Reid's account risks slipping into dogmatism because it builds so many unrevisable beliefs into us. My concern was largely motivated by his remarks about God and the force of the example involving the Idomenians. I would like now to temper that charge for several reasons.

First, Reid does not just offer the nativism as a substitute for an epistemological argument, a fact which is even clearer in the *Essays* than in the *Inquiry*, as Baruch Brody has noted. [16] Reid offers, in both the *Inquiry* and the *Essays*, additional, non-nativist arguments to back his claim that some principles must be accepted intuitively as first principles without further justification, and his position is not just a bald appeal to nativism.

Second, at least with regard to his nativist claims about con-

cept formation, Reid's position may be about as good as we can
do, at least ultimately. Roderick Chisolm argues this point in his
review of my book in *Philosophia*.[17] In Chapter V, I claim that
Reid too hastily retreats under the umbrella of nativism, as soon
as he shows that associationist learning theory cannot account for
our forming certain fundamental concepts, e.g., of the primary
qualities. Chisolm argues that "Reid points out that *any* adequate
answer to the question, 'How do we acquire our concepts?' must
fall back sooner or later upon some fundamental 'law of our constitution'."[18] When Reid points out "an original principle of our
constitution" as the explanation for why we form the concept of
solidity after being exposed to certain sensations (or to certain
material impressions), Chisolm urges he is doing the only thing
we can do:

> What Daniels fails to see is that *no* adequate theory of con-
> cepts can enable us to avoid this type of answer. Let his
> own theory be this: "We come to acquire the concept of so-
> lidity by doing so-and-so (or by experiencing such-and-such)
> [where this is an improvement on associationist learning the-
> ory]." How will *he* answer the further question: "But how is
> it that doing so-and-so (or experiencing such-and-such) can
> cause one to acquire the concept of solidity?" It is likely that
> he, too, will have to retreat under Reid's "It is an original
> principle of our constitution"—or "They just do."[19]

Even if Chisolm is right that that is the best we can ultimately do, it is not clear to me that Reid really believed it is the
best we can do. He generally believed that further scientific inquiry could yield a superior answer to the account he rejects
when he attacks the Ideal System, as I suggest in Chapter V. He
thought, as I do, that we would gain useful knowledge by pursuing that better account, even if ultimately we would have to
admit that it is just a basic fact about our constitution that it is
governed by the laws it is. Nevertheless, I believe the charge that
Reid retreats too quickly into nativism echoes and reinforces my
charge of dogmatism, and I want to soften that judgment.

My third reason for wanting to soften that charge is that it
undercuts one of the central contentions of the book as a whole.
I place Reid squarely in a tradition of 'natural philosophy': I

portrayed him as a scientist of the mind, which is how he saw himself. In rejecting the Ideal System, he was rejecting a false theory of the workings of the mind, not a method for undertaking philosophical inquiry. Seen in this light, Hume and Reid share a general approach, despite the dispute about the Ideal System.[20] Specifically, if his work is seen as a precursor to recent work in cognitive psychology and "naturalized epistemology," Reid's nativism acquires a more programmatic and less dogmatic hue.[21]

In his discussion of primary and secondary qualities, Keith Lehrer suggests one way to recast Reid's nativism in this light.[22] Reid wants to be a realist about both kinds of qualities. Why then does he want to preserve a distinction which seemed important to philosophers, such as Locke, who wanted to assign a different status to each kind of quality? Lehrer suggests that Reid thought we formed different conceptions of these types of qualities "by our constitution": we form clear and distinct conceptions of primary qualities but not of secondary qualities. Secondary qualities must be studied further through scientific inquiry for us to improve on our naturally given conceptions. (In Chapters IV and V, I argue for a similar account.) Lehrer notes Reid's theistic account of how our conceptions of these qualities arise: "Reid remarks, 'What is necessary for the conduct of our animal life, the bountiful Author of Nature hath made manifest to all men.'"[23] Lehrer then suggests we recast Reid's account, substituting

> the struggle for survival for the actions of God and what is necessary for the survival of species for what is necessary for the conduct of our animal life. We can then readily convert Reid's thesis that our senses immediately give rise to our conceptions of certain qualities to the thesis that these conceptions arise in this way because of biological imprinting having survival value for the species. In this way, the doctrine becomes a contemporary conjecture,[24]

for which Lehrer thinks there is some empirical evidence. Presumably, if we make a similar substitution regarding the rest of Reid's claims about what we get "by our constitution," we would have an even more elaborate (though perhaps less likely) contemporary conjecture.

There is another level at which Reid's appeal to nativism

has a contemporary flavor—his use of what might be called an "input-output" argument to establish the nativism. Reid, as I argue in Chapters IV and V, offers us "experiments" intended to show that tactile sensations, combined with associationist mechanisms, cannot generate our concepts of primary qualities, like extension, figure, and motion: "Our philosophers have imposed upon themselves and upon us, in pretending to deduce from sensation the first origin of our notions of external existences, of space, motion, and extension and all the primary qualities of body—that is, the qualities whereof we have the most clear and distinct conception." [25] This argument and its explicit conclusion should leave no doubt that Reid is rejecting the associationist theory of concept formation and not just its view of concept application. He leaves room, as he makes clear at other points, for the view that tactile sensations may play a role in concept application. They may serve as "signs" that signify when we can apply primary-quality concepts. But these sensations and the associationist mechanisms that operate on them cannot be the means by which we develop these concepts.

The structure of Reid's argument is similar to some contemporary arguments about nativism in language acquisition. Noam Chomsky and Jerrold Katz[26] have argued that we should investigate the properties of our language-acquisition system by seeing what features it must have in order to account for our ability to derive a particular "output," our mastery of the grammar of a language, from a particular "input," the limited language-learning contexts we are exposed to as infants. Their contention is that associationist and reinforcement mechanisms, or more generally, any sort of built-in general induction machine, will not have adequate information available in our normal language-learning contexts to generate the grammars that describe our languages. So we must suppose that our language-acquisition system natively has a built-in bias, in the form of specific mechanisms, in favor of our learning languages that share certain grammatical properties.

Reid argues in a similar fashion, on my analysis of his claim about concepts we have by our constitution. He also suggests that we must investigate the properties of our concept-acquisition system by comparing the output of that system, our concepts of primary qualities, with the available inputs, presumably our visual, tactual, and other sensations. Reid's argument then is equivalent to the claim that associationist mechanisms are not capable of generating the observed output from the observed input. In the face of this argument, Reid turns to the alternative view that there must be features of our constitution, as yet unknown to us, that enable us to derive the concepts we have from our interaction with the world.[27]

I have offered several reasons for wanting to soften my earlier charge that Reid's nativism may incline him toward dogmatism. The reader will have to make up her own mind whether this softening is reasonable or excessive charity.

Notes

Introduction

[1] Some scholars may object to my following Reid here in claiming that concepts have to resemble sensations or sensible qualities. It may be possible to interpret Berkeley as follows: His "notions" (concepts) are *produced* by sensations that are, or resemble, real qualities, but the "notions" need not *bear a resembling relation* themselves. As we shall see in Chapter IV, this interpretation does not save Berkeley from Reid's central criticism.

[2] Thomas Reid, *Inquiry into the Human Mind*, in *Reid's Works*, Dugald Stewart, ed., Vol. I, (Charlestown: Samuel Etheridge, 1813), p. 275.

[3] *Ibid.*, p. 284.

[4] Cf. Note 1, above, and also Chapter IV, Sect. I and 2.

Chapter I

[1] Reid's "Geometry of Visibles" was first pointed out to me by Professor Hilary Putnam. The first written reference I found to Reid's non-Euclidean geometry is in D.M.Y. Sommerville *Elements of Non-Euclidean Geometry* (London: G. Bell and Sons, Ltd., 1914). Professor Dirk Struik has recently informed me that Reid's discovery was first brought to the attention of the mathematical community by J. Cockle, "On the Confluence and Bifurcation of Certain Theories," *Proceedings London Mathematical Society*, 20 (1889) p. 4-17 (also, *Nature*, vol 39, 1889, pp. 521-523) in 1889. D.M.Y. Sommerville's mention of Reid derives from Cockle's rediscovery. Reid's achievement subsequently fell completely from view.

[2] It seems unlikely that Reid was aware of Saccheri's work, which, in spite of the attention it attracted on publication, was for the most part soon forgotten and did not appear in English until 1894 (cf. Roberto Bonola, *Non-Euclidean Geometry: A Critical and Historical Study of Its Development*, Carslow, H.S., trans. (Chicago: Open Court Publishing Co., 1912), p. 44). Reid did, however have an interest in mathematics dating from his youth and lectured on "Euclid's Axioms and Definitions" as late as 1761-1762. Cf. A. Campbell Fraser, *Thomas Reid*, Famous Scots Series (Edinburgh: Olephant, Anderson and Gerries, 1898), p. 53.

[3] Treatises on spherical trigonometry were written in the 18th century and were often appended to editions of Euclid's *Elements*. For example, Dr. John Keil appended such a treatise to an edition of 1781. Keil's Proposition I, "Great circles ACB, AFB, mutually bisect each other" and XV, "Equiangular spherical triangles are also equilateral" are explicitly about curved lines in Euclidean space. In contrast,

Reid speaks of "Right lines" and "right-lined triangles" in the analogous theorems of his geometry of visibles. Cf. *Elements of Euclid,* Robert Simson, ed., trans., 6th ed. (Edinburgh: J. Balfour, 1781).

[4] Reid, *Inquiry,* p. 293.

[5] *Ibid.,* p. 291.

[6] *Euclid's Elements,* John Keil, ed. (London, 1733), p.l.

[7] Reid's, *Inquiry,* pp. 290-297.

[8] *Ibid.,* p. 291. Reid also says that "[E]very the least part of space bears a finite *ratio* to the whole. So that with them the whole extent of space is the common and natural measure of every thing that hath length and breadth, and the magnitude of every body and of every figure is expressed by its being such a part of the universe. In like manner, the common and natural measure of length, is an infinite right line, which, as hath been before observed, returns into itself, and hath no limits, but bears a finite *ratio* to every other line." (*Ibid.,* p. 299).

[9] *Ibid.,* p. 281.

[10] George Berkeley, *An Essay Towards A New Theory of Vision,* in *The Works of George Berkeley, Bishop of Cloyne,* Vol. I, Luce, A.A. and Jessup., T.E., ed. (London: Thomas Nelson and Sons, 1953) Sect. 61.

[11] Some contemporary research has tried to establish that the geometry appropriate to visual perception is really a hyperbolic geometry. See for example, R. H. Lunenburg's *Mathematical Analysis of Binocular Vision* (Princeton: 1947), and A. A. Blank, articles in *British Journal of Physiological Optics,* July and October 1957, pp. 1-29, and *Journal of Optical Society of America,* Vol 43, No. 9, pp. 717-727 (1953), and Vol. 48, No. 12, pp. 911-925 (1958). Professor R. B. Angell has recently shown me an unpublished paper in which he argues that visual space is doubly elliptical, as Reid contends.

[12] Reid, *Inquiry,* p. 291.

[13] Reid seems to take "infinite" to mean "hath no limits": "the common and natural measure of length, is an infinite right line, which, as hath been before observed, returns into itself, and hath no limits, but bears a finite *ratio* to every other line." (*Ibid.,* p. 299).

[14] There is a slight problem with our account of visibles in the next section as it relates to Reid's claim: if visibles are equivalence classes, it is odd to talk of their projections onto a sphere. We could, however, at the risk of abandoning our interpretation, imagine selecting members of each equivalence class of points of an appropriate sphere.

[15] *Ibid.,* p. 292.

[16] *Ibid.,* 293.

[17] *Ibid.*, p. 292.

[18] *Ibid.*, p. 280.

[19] *Ibid.*, p. 288.

[20] *Ibid.*, p. 280.

[21] *Ibid.*, pp. 293-294.

[22] *Ibid.*, p. 293.

[23] *Ibid.*, p. 294.

[24] *Ibid.*, pp. 290, 294.

[25] *Ibid.*, pp. 288-290.

[26] *Ibid.*, p. 294.

[27] *Ibid.*, p. 288.

[28] *Ibid.*

[29] *Ibid.*, p. 282.

[30] *Ibid.*, p. 281.

[31] *Ibid.*, p. 282.

[32] Edwin Abbott Abbott, *Flatland; A Romance of Many Dimensions by A²* (London: Seeley, 1884).

[33] Reid, *Inquiry*, p. 301.

[34] Carl Friedrich Gauss, *Werke* (Gottingen: B. G. Teubner, 1900), Vol. VIII, p. 187. Translations are my own. See note 43, Ch. I, for a discussion of "constant proportionality."

[35] *Ibid.*, p. 177.

[36] *Ibid.*, p. 224.

[37] The commonly held view that the work of Gauss, Bolyai, and Lobachevsky was carried out as an "uninterpreted" system is not incompatible with what is claimed above. All that is meant is that there was an obvious intended interpretation of the geometrical sentences used in their arguments, namely, the same physical

interpretation normally associated with Euclidean geometry. Negating the parallels postulate and using it in proofs as one would an "uninterpreted" sentence is not incompatible with thinking that there is an intended interpretation and, further, with thinking that on that interpretation, the parallels postulate and its negation will contain non-logical terms with the same meaning.

[38] Nicholai Lobachevsky, "The Introduction to Lobachevsky's *New Elements of Geometry*," trans. G. B. Halstead, extract from a paper presented to the Texas Academy of Sciences, Dec. 22, 1897.

[39] Nicholai Lobachevsky, *Geometrical Researches on the Theory of Parallels* (1840), G. B. Halstead, trans., (Austin: Univ. of Texas, 1891), p. 44-45.

[40] For a more complete discussion of these views of Lobachevsky and the sense in which they anticipate later work on the relation between geometry and physics, see my article, "Lobachevsky: Some Anticipations of Later Views on the Relation between Geometry and Physics," *ISSIS*, (forthcoming, 1975). See also, V. Kagan, *N. Lobachevsky and his Contribution to Science* (Moscow: Foreign Languages Publishing House, 1957).

[41] In the 18th century, a particular strategy, using a *reductio ad absurdum* form, became prominent in the effort to determine the status of the fifth (parallels) Euclidean postulate. The Euclidean axiom system is modified by replacing the fifth postulate with its negation (or the equivalent). Then, if the fifth postulate is not independent of the other axioms, systematic deductions from the modified system should generate contradictions. Of course, failure to generate a contradiction would itself be no proof of independence. The development of this strategy proved to be of primary importance in advancing the theory of parallels. The strategy closed off unpromising lines of attack and permitted extensive development of would-be alternatives without forcing an early decision about consistency. Further, independent researchers who learned of the basic strategy were able to rediscover key facts, with the result that a minimum of communication between researchers could still lead to a maximum sharing of knowledge. In such a setting, it is not so surprising that at least three men, Gauss, Lobachevsky, and Bolyai, reached similar conclusions independently, and several others came very close. Whatever tributes one may want to pay to individual genius, nevertheless, theoretical advance in geometry emerged out of a community of mathematicians practicing within a definite tradition of problem-solving activity. What makes Reid's discovery so unusual is that he stands completely outside this community and its tradition. For a fuller discussion of this early work on alternative geometries, see Bonola, *Non-Euclidean Geometry*.

[42] Lambert used as his basic construction in investigating the theory of parallels a three right-angled quadrilateral and made three hypotheses about the nature of the fourth angle. In his *reductio* strategy, the goal was to eliminate the Obtuse Angle Hypothesis (equivalent to Riemannian geometry) and the Acute Angle Hypothesis (Lobachevskian), leaving only the Right Angle (Euclidean) Hypothesis. The Obtuse Angle Hypothesis was thought to be eliminable because proofs made no distinction between infinite and unbounded planes.

Lambert remarked that a geometry developed on the Hypothesis of the
Obtuse Angle would have a close resemblance to spherical geometry and that a
geometry developed on the Hypothesis of the Acute Angle would occur in the case
of an imaginary sphere. Lambert may have been led to his second remark as
follows: the area of a plane triangle on the Hypothesis of the Acute Angle is given
by $r^2(\Pi-A-B-C)$. We can derive this formula from $(A+B+C-\Pi)r^2$, the area
of a spherical triangle, by substituting the imaginary radius $r\sqrt{-1}$ for r. Cf.
Johann Heinrich Lambert, *Theorie der Parallel-Linien* (1766); also, Bonola,
Non-Euclidean Geometry.

Sixty years later, in the course of developing his new, "imaginary" geometry,
Lobachevsky noted:

> If someone wants therefore to suppose now that somewhere in the
> consequences there will be a contradiction, to the repudiation of the
> elements which we have supposed in the new geometry, then this
> contradiction must already stand in the equation. Yet we notice that
> these equations turn into the equations of spherical trigonometry as
> soon as we substitute $a\sqrt{-1}$, $b\sqrt{-1}$, $c\sqrt{-1}$ for a, b, c; however, in the
> customary geometry and in spherical trigonometry we meet only the
> experience of lines; consequently the customary geometry, spherical
> trigonometry and this new geometry will always be in accord. ("Ueber
> die Anfangsgrunde der Geometrie," (1829) in *Zwei Geometrische
> Abhandlungen,* p. 65.)

Lobachevsky's remark here is intended to make it seem plausible that his new
geometry is consistent if spherical trigonometry is. It is the sketch of an analytic
proof of relative consistency, but he never completes it. For example, it is not in-
general the case that every equation that has solutions for pure imaginary values of
its variables will have solutions for real values of its variables. Although $a^2 = -1$ has
no solution for real values of a, if we substitute $a\sqrt{-1}$ for a to get $a^2 = 1$, we get an
equation with solutions for real values of a. Lobachevsky would have to show that
no such difficulty arises in the case of the equations central to his geometry, which
he does not bother to do. Nevertheless, it is rather impressive that as early as 1829
he had begun to think in terms of proving relative consistency, a project generally
thought by historians of mathematics to have been undertaken somewhat later in
the 19th century by other mathematicians.

[43] One sharply counter-intuitive feature of the new geometry—the possibility that
there might exist an absolute unit of length—was first noted by Johann Heinrich
Lambert in his *Theorie der Parallel-Linien* (1766). In ordinary (Euclidean) geometry,
measurement of lines is clearly "relative" in the following sense: there are no
functions which permit the expression of the length of a line segment in terms of
certain "fundamental" figures, like straight lines, planes, or pencils. On the other
hand, we can measure an angle in Euclidean geometry by considering its ratio to a
complete revolution (the entire pencil), and so angle measurement is "absolute."
On the geometry following from the Hypothesis of the Acute angle (see note 42
above), Lambert was able to associate a definite angle with every segment. An
appropriate function of the associated angles gives us the needed properties for
measuring lines, and in particular, we can take as the absolute unit of length the
segment for which this function takes the value 1. Because Lambert thought such
an absolute measure was intuitively impossible, he was inclined to reject the
possibility of this new geometry, although he never felt he could prove such an
absolute measure to be a contradiction.

Chapter II

¹ John Locke, *An Essay Concerning Human Understanding*, Alexander Campbell Fraser, ed., Two Volumes (New York: Dover, 1959), Vol. I, p. 32.

² These remarks should not be taken to mean, for example, that we cannot find a special problem for the philosophy of science in Hume's discussion of induction. Hume's own discussion, however, had the skeptical bite it did because the framework of the problem was restricted by the theory of mind he was developing.

³ Thomas Reid, *Inquiry*, p. 172.

⁴ *Ibid.*, p. 329-330.

⁵ Douglas Sloan, *The Scottish Enlightenment and the American College Ideal* (Teachers College Press, 1971), p. 22.

⁶ Reid was known as a Moderate Clergyman. The Moderate Clergy wanted to reconcile science and the interests of religion. In fact, they wanted to show they were necessary to one another. In a sense, then, Reid's quarrel with Berkeley was really a squabble within the Church about *how* to reconcile religion with science—through idealism and phenomenalism or through a dogmatic realism. Some of the Moderate Clergy, although not in particular Reid, shared with Berkeley the view that materialism was the real enemy, for 18th-century materialism had attacked theology extensively. Cf. Sloan, *The Scottish Enlightenment*, p. 13-14.

⁷ Berkeley's remarks about scientific laws can be found in his *Three Dialogues between Hylas and Philonous, The Principles of Human Knowledge,* and especially in *De Motu*. Cf. *The Works of George Berkeley, Bishop of Cloyne,* A. A. Luce and T. E. Jessup, eds., Nine Volumes (Edinburgh: Nelson and Sons, 1948-1957).

⁸ René Descartes, "Dioptrics." *Philosophical Writings,* a selection edited and translated by Elizabeth Anscombe and Peter Geach (Edinburgh: Nelson, 1954), p. 249.

⁹ Descartes, "Dioptrics" p. 250.

¹⁰ His influence on Berkeley is well documented in A. A. Luce, *Berkeley and Malebranche: A Study in the Origins of Berkeley's Thought* (London: Oxford University Press, 1934), Cf. especially Chapter II, "Theories of Vision."

¹¹ Malebranche, *Search after Truth: or a Treatise of the Nature of the Human Mind and of its Management for Avoiding Error in the Sciences,* Richard Sault, trans. (London: J. Dunton, 1694), I, p. 47. In fact, in order not to be fooled by terminology, we might note that natural judgments are *compound* whereas Descartes' calculation by natural geometry is a *simple* act of the imagination. This terminological disagreement does not seem to mean much.

[12] Malebranche, *Search*, p. 47.

[13] *Ibid.*, Chap. IX.

[14] The edition of Malebranche from which the diagram and passage are quoted was translated into English and published in London in 1694. Not only were both Berkeley and Porterfield familiar in general with Malebranche's work, but it is also extremely likely that Reid had seen these passages in particular, since he had read Malebranche extensively. Cf. *Inquiry*, p. 180.

[15] Malebranche, *Search*, pp. 54-55.

[16] Molyneux, *Dioptrics Nova: A Treatise of Dioptrick* (London, 1692), p. 113.

[17] *Ibid.*, p. 113.

[18] *Ibid.*

[19] Berkeley, *New Theory of Vision.* § 10, emphasis added.

[20] All that is meant by the phrase, "the eye itself cannot do X," on my interpretation of 18th century theory of vision, is that information which has its origin in the retina is not a sufficient input to the brain to permit the exercise or development of certain abilities, say, distance discrimination abilities. Rather, some other input, like tactual sensations, must be coordinated with the information deriving from the "impression" on the retina, which requires the exercise of some other deep process in addition to whatever deep processes work on purely retinal inputs.

[21] Berkeley, *New Theory of Vision,* § 50.

[22] See discussion of point (g), Chapter I, above.

[23] Porterfield, *A Treatise on the Eye: The Manner and Phenomena of Vision* (Edinburgh: 1759), I, p. 372.

[24] James Jurin, "An Essay upon Distinct and Indistinct Vision," printed in Robert Smith, *A Compleat System of Optiks* (Cambridge: Cornelius Crownfield, 1738), Vol. II.

[25] Smith, *Compleat System*, Vol. I.

[26] Both Smith and Reid seem unaware of constancy scaling phenomena.

[27] Porterfield, *Treatise on the Eye,* Vols. I, II. Reid refers to Porterfield in several important sections on vision.

[28] Porterfield, *Treatise on the Eye*, II, p. 8. A generous interpretation might ascribe to Porterfield awareness of the manner in which servo-mechanism comes to operate here.

²⁹ *Ibid.*, p. 16.

³⁰ "thro' vulgarity, in a loose figurative and improper speech, we say that the motion of the pupil, the uniform motions of our eyes, the vital and natural motions, are necessary, involuntary, not under the power and domination of our will; yet in truth and in strictness of speaking, as they are all caused by the volitions of the mind, they must necessarily be both voluntary and free, and, of consequence intirely subject to the power and influence of this active principle; for I think a necessary agent, or necessary action, is a contradiction in terms; for whatever acts necessarily, does not indeed act at all, but is only acted upon; is not an agent at all, but a mere patient." *Ibid..* p. 151.

³¹ *Ibid.,* p. 8.

³² *Ibid.,* p. 17.

³³ *Ibid.,* p. 22.

³⁴ *Ibid.,* p. 120.

³⁵ *Ibid.,* p. 136.

³⁶ Reid, *Inquiry,* p. 391.

³⁷ *Ibid.,* pp. 391-392.

³⁸ *Ibid.,* p. 398.

³⁹ *Ibid.*

Chapter III

¹ Cf. *Phil Com* §101, Notebook B, in which Berkeley first suggests the problem: "Geometry seems to have for its object tangible extension, figure, and motion, and not visible." Berkeley, *Works,* I, p. 17.

² *Ibid,* p. 186-187. Reid attacks this Berkeleyan position in the Argument for Independence of Color and Figure, discussed in Ch. IV, Sec. 3.

³ It is not my concern here to comment on what sense can be made of Berkeley's distinction between objects "in the mind" or "external" to the mind, or on the validity of his argument about the impossibility of separating "color" and "figure" "in thought." As I show in Chapter IV, Reid replies to this argument of Berkeley in the *Inquiry* by designing a thought experiment intended to show that a modified eye might perceive visible figure without any sensations of color.

⁴ Some commentators, such as A. A. Luce, have argued convincingly that Berkeley was a full-blown immaterialist when he wrote *New Theory of Vision.* They argue he

took his "halfway" position for tactical reasons, believing it would be tactically easier to make a successful case for vision if touch were not attempted at the same time.

5 Berkeley, *New Theory of Vision*, § 147.

6 A. A. Luce makes a partial denial of this claim: "in the *Principles* (§44) and in *Theory of Vision Vindicated* (§35) Berkeley still maintains the heterogeneity, and he can do so; for visible and tangible being different objects of different senses obviously must differ; but in both these works the doctrine has lost all its old importance and much of its meaning. Now visible and tangible are both sense data . . . they belong to the same genus, and so they are not, strictly, heterogeneous." Berkeley, *Works*, p. 151.

7 Reid, *Inquiry*, p. 294. Reid also remarks that we find it very difficult to attend carefully to the visible figure and consequently have not noticed its properties differ from tangible figure—we never notice the "sign" but attend only to the "thing signified."

8 *Ibid.*, p. 294-295.

9 *Ibid.*, p. 290.

10 *Ibid.*, p. 281.

11 *Ibid.*

12 Cf. feature (f) described in Chapter I, above.

13 Berkeley, *New Theory of Vision*, p. 233.

14 Reid, *Inquiry*, p. 295.

15 Such thought experiments, often variations on the Molyneux problem, were common investigative tools of 18th-century researchers in the theory of mind. Their main function was to isolate necessary and sufficient conditions for the development or "derivation" of a given idea, concept, or ability. Whenever possible, actual medical cases were looked for which might settle the relevant question empirically. Often, however, these medical cases lacked many relevant controls, itself a reflection of the rather undeveloped nature of the background theory that suggested the problems in the first place.

16 Berkeley, *New Theory of Vision*, § 154.

17 Reid, *Inquiry*, p. 295.

18 *Ibid.*, pp. 296-297.

19 Berkeley, *New Theory of Vision*, §155.

Chapter IV

[1] Reid, *Inquiry*, p. 248.

[2] *Ibid.*, p. 274-275.

[3] *Ibid.*

[4] *Ibid.*

[5] *Ibid.*, p. 284.

[6] *Ibid.*, p. 254.

[7] *Ibid.*, p. 276.

[8] *Ibid.*, p. 278.

[9] I owe the suggestion of this way of reconstructing Berkeley's argument to Hilary Putnam.

[10] Cf., "[T]he ideas of secondary qualities are no resemblances. . . . If the qualities of body were known to us only by sensations that resemble them, then color, and sound, and heat, could be no qualities of body." (Reid, *Inquiry*, pp. 277-278).

[11] The idealist may still try to save a version of the "resemblance" thesis contained in H1 and H2 by saying that concepts are derived from sensations that resemble them. Concepts apply to these sensations *because* they resemble them. For Reid, however, the world contains both qualities and sensations. Since Reid thinks H2 is true, and we can assume the resemblance relation is transitive, then if concepts resemble corresponding sensations, they cannot resemble qualities. Consequently, the original explanatory value of the resemblance thesis disappears and the door is open to an attack on the analysis of "having a concept" advanced in H1.

[12] *Ibid.*, p. 279.

[13] *Ibid.*, p. 267.

[14] *Ibid.*, pp. 268, 270.

[15] *Ibid.*, p. 270.

[16] *Ibid.*, p. 271.

[17] *Ibid.*, p. 284.

[18] Cf. *Ibid.*, pp. 236-237.

[19] *Ibid.*, pp. 268-269.

[20] Reid shows awareness of such possibilities in several places: "no man can be sure that it [scarlet] affects his eye in the same manner as it affects the eye of another, and that it has the same appearance to him as it has to another man." (*Inquiry*, p. 280). Also, "It is impossible to know whether a scarlet color has the same appearance to me which it hath to another man: and if the appearances of it to different persons differed as much as color does from sound, they might never be able to discover this difference". (*Ibid.*, p. 260). Reid thus seems to be out of sympathy with the verificationist who might claim this supposition is "meaningless." The supposition of systematically different sensations does not seem to be unverifiable if we could develop an adequate psycho-physiological theory and detect relevent differences between types of perceivers.

[21] *Ibid.*, p. 236.

[22] *Ibid.*, p. 228.

[23] *Ibid.*, p. 236.

[24] A "definition" here will simply be an accurate statement of our conception of a given quality.

[25] We will omit discussion of motion.

[26] Reid, *Inquiry*, p. 237.

[27] We can speak loosely of "defined" and "primitive" *concepts* rather than terms.

[28] Reid, *Inquiry*, p. 238.

[29] *Ibid.*, p. 238.

[30] *Ibid.*, p. 285.

[31] *Ibid.*, pp. 285-286.

[32] *Ibid.*, p. 286, emphasis added.

[33] *Ibid.*, p. 288.

[34] *Ibid.*

[35] *Ibid.*, pp. 241-242.

[36] *Ibid.*, p. 259.

[37] *Ibid.* Dr. Saunderson was a blind mathematician living in the 18th century.

[38] *Ibid.*, p. 280.

[39] *Ibid.*, p. 281.

[40] X and y have the same position with regard to the eye if x and y lie in the same right line drawn from the center of the eye. The degree of difference of position gives Reid his metric.

[41] Reid, *Inquiry*, p. 283.

[42] Berkeley, *New Theory of Vision*, §43.

Chapter V

[1] Reid, *Inquiry*, pp. 302-303.

[2] Porterfield, *Treatise on the Eye*, II, p. 372.

[3] Reid, *Inquiry*, p. 303.

[4] *Ibid.*, p. 313.

[5] *Ibid.*, p. 361.

[6] *Ibid.*, p. 304.

[7] Porterfield, *Treatise on the Eye*, I, pp. 114-115.

[8] Reid, *Inquiry*, p. 355.

[9] *Ibid.*, p. 172.

[10] *Ibid.*, p. 329.

[11] *Ibid.*, p. 236.

[12] *Ibid.*, p. 251.

[13] *Ibid.*, p. 355.

[14] *Ibid.*, pp. 250, 383.

[15] *Ibid.*, p. 199.

[16] *Ibid.*, p. 240, emphasis added. At first it might seem that Reid here contradicts our argument for "no special sensations" (cf. Chapter IV), since he seems to tie the

concepts of hardness to certain tactual sensations "by our constitution." There is no contradiction. The sensations we have by pressing a hard body are not special sensations, ones "semantically tied" to our concept of hardness. That is, they are not sensations which must be referred to when we state our conception of hardness. I say in Chapter IV that the theory of concept formation Reid was attacking required just such special sensations. Further, I show Reid argues (in a thought experiment) that our sensations of touch can *not* give rise to any clear and distinct conceptions of primary qualities *if we rely only on introspectible information on those sensations.*

[17] Cf. Chapter IV, Note 27. Further, as was pointed out in Chapter IV, Reid has no way of explicating the clarity of our concepts of the primitives, such as force and position (cf. Chapter IV, p. 80.).

[18] Reid, *Inquiry*, p. 240.

[19] *Ibid.*, p. 207.

[20] *Ibid.*

[21] *Ibid.*, p. 221.

[22] Cf. Chapter II.

[23] Reid, *Inquiry*, p. 207.

[24] *Ibid.*, pp. 250-251. Also cf. *Ibid.*, p. 174, for a distinction between two types of natively endowed powers, some which do and some which do not depend on "human culture . . . and exercise" for their development.

[25] Reid, *Inquiry*, pp. 241-242.

[26] *Ibid.*, p. 243.

[27] *Ibid.*

[28] *Ibid.*, pp. 243-244.

[29] *Ibid.*, p. 250.

[30] *Ibid.*, p. 235.

[31] *Ibid.*, p. 205.

[32] *Ibid.*, p. 250.

[33] *Ibid.*, p. 247.

[34] *Ibid.*, p. 236., emphasis added.

[35] *Ibid.*, p. 250.

[36] *Ibid.*, p. 172.

[37] *Ibid.*, pp. 221, 234.

[38] *Ibid.*, pp. 207, 227.

[39] *Ibid.*, p. 250.

[40] *Ibid.*, pp. 234, 250, 416, 418.

[41] *Ibid.*, p. 252.

[42] Porterfield, *Treatise on the Eye*, II, p. 364.

[43] Of course, the interaction is reciprocal. In this case, both alternatives, the idealist skepticism and the realist nativism, probably were harmful influences on scientific practice in 18th-century theory of vision.

[44] Reid, *Inquiry*, p. 193.

[45] *Ibid.*, p. 194.

[46] *Ibid.*, pp. 412-413.

[47] Cf. *Ibid.*, pp. 295-297.

[48] Cf. *Ibid.*, p. 199.

[49] *Ibid.*, p. 297.

[50] *Ibid.*, p. 250.

[51] I have discussed why visual space is two-dimensional in Chapters I and II.

[52] Reid, *Inquiry.*, p. 297.

[53] *Ibid.*, p. 296.

[54] *Ibid.*, p. 299.

[55] Cf. Chapter V, Section 2.

[56] Reid, *Inquiry*, p. 295.

[57] *Ibid.*, p. 250.

⁵⁸ *Ibid.*

⁵⁹ *Ibid.*

⁶⁰ *Ibid.*

⁶¹ *Ibid.*, pp. 440-441.

⁶² *Ibid.*, p. 440.

⁶³ *Ibid.*, p. 301.

⁶⁴ *Ibid.*, p. 295.

⁶⁵ I ignore the objection that the Idomenians and humans have no disagreement since they mean different things by "body."

⁶⁶ Reid, *Inquiry*, p. 250.

⁶⁷ *Ibid.*, p. 245.

⁶⁸ "The victory of the Moderates was highly significant in shaping the expression and determining the direction of Enlightenment thought in Scotland. The Moderates were determined to show that the cause of science, progress and genteel culture and the interests of religion were not only compatible, but also necessary to one another. The result was that in Scotland the potential for conflict between the forces of enlightenment and of religion was greatly lessened . . . *E' crasez l' enfame* was never a Scottish slogan, even among those who, like David Hume and Adam Smith, held the most tenuous relationships with the Church and were close friends of such persons as Voltaire, d'Holbach, Rousseau, and other fairly radical continentals." (Sloan, *The Scottish Enlightenment*, pp. 13-14).

⁶⁹ *Ibid.*, p. 129.

⁷⁰ *Ibid.*, p. 130.

⁷¹ *Ibid.*, p. 155.

⁷² Here, for example, are Smith's "five rules" of scientific method:
1. "That no law should be admitted on hypothesis, but should rest solely on an induction of facts."
2. "That laws collected from an ample and accurate induction of facts should be deemed universal, till other facts occur to invalidate, or limit the conclusions which have been drawn from them."
3. "That laws founded on a partial induction of facts should not be extended beyond the limits to which they are certainly known to apply."
4. "That similar appearances should, because of the uniformity of nature, be referred, as far as possible to the same causes."
5. "That the testimony of our senses, and of all our simple perceptions ought to be

admitted as true, and no ulterior evidence be required of the reality, or the nature of the facts which they confirm." (From Smith's *Lectures on Subjects of Moral and Political Philosophy* (2 vol., Trenton, N.J.), quoted in Sloan, *The Scottish Enlightenment,* p. 159).

[73] For a more complete discussion of Reid's influence in America, see a doctoral dissertation by Richard J. Petersen, "Scottish Common Sense in America, 1768-1850: An Evaluation of its influence" (American University, 1963).

Afterword

[1] See the reviews of my book by Baruch Brody in *Journal of Philosophy* 73 (1): 25-27; Roderick Chisolm in *Philosophia* 13 (1-2): 81-84; and P. V. in *Review of Metaphysics* 30 (1977): 759-760.

[2] David Fate Norton, "Reid's Abstract of the *Inquiry into the Human Mind,*" in Stephen F. Barker and Thomas L. Beauchamp, eds., *Thomas Reid: Critical Interpretations* (Philadelphia: Philosophical Monographs, 1976), p. 131 n. 7.

[3] Susan Margaret Weldon, "Thomas Reid's Theory of Vision," Ph.D. diss., McGill University, 1978, pp. 179-181.

[4] *Ibid.,* p. 181.

[5] *Ibid.*

[6] *Ibid.*

[7] See Brody, p. 26; Chisolm, p. 82; John Immerwahr, *Journal of the History of Philosophy* 14 (1976): 371-374; W. Breidert, *Isis* 67 (3): 238 (1976): 485-486; G. N. Cantor, *Annals of Science* 32 (6): 596-597 (1975); R. G. Olson, *Historia Mathematica* 3: 486-487; G. N. Henderson, *Philosophical Books* 17 (1976): 26-28.

[8] Norton, "Reid's Abstract," p. 127.

[9] *Ibid.;* and see Duggan's "Introduction" to Thomas Reid, *Inquiry into the Human Mind,* edited by Timothy Duggan (Chicago: University of Chicago Press, 1970), p. xx.

[10] Weldon, "Thomas Reid's Theory of Vision," p. 120; see also Susan Weldon, "Direct Realism and Visual Distortion: A Development of Arguments of Thomas Reid," *Journal of the History of Philosophy* 20 (1982): 355-368.

[11] Weldon, "Thomas Reid's Theory of Vision," p. 119.

[12] John Immerwahr, "The Development of Reid's Realism," *Monist* 61 (2): 245-255.

[13] *Ibid.,* p. 249.

[14] This and the next few paragraphs draw on my "On Having Concepts 'By Our Constitution,'" in Barker and Beauchamp, *Thomas Reid: Critical Interpretations*, pp. 35-43.

[15] *An Inquiry into the Human Mind*, Chapter V, Section VII, in Thomas Reid, *Works*, vols. 1 and 2, edited by William Hamilton (Edinburgh: Maclachlan & Stewart, 1872), p. 130; in *An Inquiry into the Human Mind*, edited by Timothy Duggan, p. 82. Subsequent references to the *Inquiry* cite the Hamilton edition first, followed by cross-reference to the Duggan edition.

[16] Brody, pp. 26-27; see also P. V.; see also William Alston, "Thomas Reid on Epistemic Principles," *History of Philosophy Quarterly* 2 (4): 435-449; Paul Vernier, "Thomas Reid on the Foundations of Knowledge and his Answer to Skepticism," in Barker and Beauchamp, *Thomas Reid: Critical Interpretations*, pp. 14-24; and James G. Hanink, "Thomas Reid and Common Sense Foundationalism," *New Scholasticism* 60 (1): 91-115.

[17] Chisolm, pp. 82-84.

[18] *Ibid.*, p. 82.

[19] *Ibid.*, p. 84.

[20] Cf. Barry Stroud, *Hume*, Arguments of the Philosophers Series (London: Routledge and Kegan Paul, 1977).

[21] See John-Christian Smith, "Reid's Functional Explanation of Sensation," *History of Philosophy Quarterly* 3 (2): 175-193; and Daniel Robinson, "Thomas Reid's *Gestalt* Psychology," in Barker and Beauchamp, *Thomas Reid: Critical Interpretations*, pp. 44-54.

[22] Keith Lehrer, "Reid on Primary and Secondary Qualities," *Monist* 61 (2): 184-191.

[23] *Ibid.*, p. 190.

[24] *Ibid.*; Lehrer cites as evidence Keith Allan, "Classifiers," *Language* 53 (2): 298.

[25] *Inquiry*, Chapter V, Section VI, p. 126; Duggan, p. 75.

[26] For Chomsky, see Noam Chomsky, *Cartesian Linguistics* (New York: Harper & Row, 1966), and "Recent Contributions to the Theory of Innate Ideas," *Synthese* 17:2-11. For Katz, see Jerrold Katz, "Innate Ideas," in Stephen P. Stich, ed., *Innate Ideas* (Berkeley, Calif.: University of California Press, 1975), pp. 145-163.

[27] Reid's argument, unlike Chomsky's, might be taken to challenge the adequacy of the account of inputs rather than the adequacy of the learning mechanisms. On sensationist versions of associationism, however, both inputs and learning mechanisms will suffer the same fate. There is no account of mechanisms that operate on inputs other than sensations.

Bibliography

Abbott, Edwin A., *Flatland; A Romance in Many Dimensions by A²*, London: Seeley, 1884. (Several paperback reprints available.)

Abbott, Thomas K., *Sight and Touch: An Attempt to Disprove the Received (or Berkleian) Theory of Vision*, London: Longman, Green, Roberts, 1864.

Alexandrov, A.D., Kolomogorov, A.N., Lavrent'ev, M.A., ed., *Mathematics: Its Content, Methods, and Meaning*, Gould, S.A., Bartha, T., trans., Cambridge, Mass: MIT Press, 1963.

Berkeley, George, *Works of George Berkeley Bishop of Cloyne*, Nine Volumes, Luce, A.A., and Jessup, T.E., ed., London: Thomas Nelson and Sons, 1948-1957.

Bonola, Roberto, *Non-Euclidean Geometry: A Critical and Historical Study of its Development*, Carslow, H.S., trans., Chicago: Open Court Publishing Company, 1912.

Boring, Edwin G., *A History of Experimental Psychology*, Century Psychology Series, New York: Century Co., 1929.

————, *Sensation and Perception in the History of Experimental Psychology*, Century Psychology Series, New York: D. Appleton-Century, 1942.

Brown, Thomas, *Lectures on the Philosophy of the Human Mind*, in three volumes, Vol. I, Andover: Mark Newman, 1822.

Carnap, Rudolf, *Philosophical Foundations of Physics: An Introduction to the Philosophy Science*, Gardner, Martin, ed., New York: Basic Books, 1966.

Cockle, J., "On the Confluence and Bifurcations of Certain Theories," *Proceedings London Mathematical Society*, 20 (1889), pp. 4-17; *Nature*, Volume 39, 1889, pp. 521-523.

Daniels, Norman, "Lobachevsky: Some Anticipations of Later Views on the Relation between Geometry and Physics," *ISIS*, "Vol. 66, No. 231, Spring 1975.

————, "Thomas Reid's Discovery of a Non-Euclidean Geometry," *Philosophy of Science*, June 1972, 39: 219-234.

————, *Thomas Reid's Discovery of a Non-Euclidean Geometry: A Case Study in the Relation Between Theory and Practice*, Doctoral Dissertation, Harvard, 1970.

Descartes, René, *Philosophical Writings*, a selection edited and translated by Elizabeth Anscombe and Peter Geach, Edinburgh: Nelson, 1954.

Euclid, *Elements of Euclid,* Keil, John, ed., London: 1733.
————, *Elements of All Geometry,* Martin, Benjamin, ed., London: J. Noon, 1739.
————,*Elements of Euclid,* Simson, Robert, trans, ed., Glasgow: R. and A. Faulis, 1756. 6th edition, Edinburgh: J. Balfour, 1781.
Fraser, A. Campbell, *Thomas Reid,* Famous Scots Series, Edinburgh: Olephant, Anderson and Ferrier, 1898.
Gauss, Carl Freidrich, *Werke,* Vol. III, Gottingen: B. G. Teubner, 1900.
Kagan, V. N., *Lobachevsky and his Contribution to Science,* Moscow: Foreign Languages Publishing House, 1957.
Lobachevsky, Nikolai I., *Geometrical Researchers on the Theory of Parallels* (1840) Halstead G. B., trans., Austin: University of Texas, 1891.
————, "New Elements of Geometry," "The Introduction to Lobachevsky's New Elements of Geometry," trans. Halstead. Extract from a paper presented to the Texas Academy of Sciences, Dec. 22, 1897.
————, *Pangeometrie* (1856), Liebmann, Heinrich, trans. (German), Ostwald's Klassiker der Exakten Wissenschaften, Leipzig: Wilhelm Engelman, 1902.
————, *Zwei Geometrische Abhandlungen,* Engel, Friedrich, trans., Vol. I, Leipzig: B. G. Teubner, 1898.
Locke, John, *An Essay Concerning the Understanding, Knowledge, Opinion, and Assent,* Rand, Benjamin, ed., Cambridge: Harvard University Press, 1931.
Luce, A.A., *Berkeley and Malebranche: A Study in the Origin of Berkeley's Thought,* London: Oxford University Press, 1934.
Lunenburg, R.H., *Mathematical Analysis of Binocular Vision,* Princeton: 1947.
Malebranche, Nicolas, *Search After Truth: or a Treatise of the Nature of the Human Mind and of its Management for Avoiding Error in the Sciences,* Vol. I, II, London: J. Dunton, 1694.
Maseves, Francis, ed., *Scriptores Optici; or A Collection of Tracts Relating to Optics,* London: R. Wilks, 1823.
Molyneux, William, *Dioptrics Nova: A Treatise of Dioptrick,* London, 1692.
Pogorelov, A.V., *Lectures on the Foundations of Geometry,* Boron, L.F., Bouwsma, W.D., trans., Netherlands: P. Noordhoff, 1966.
Porterfield, William, *Treatise on the Eye: the Manner and Phenomena of Vision,* Edinburgh: 1759.

Reid, Thomas, *Works,* in Four volumes, Stewart, Dugald, ed., Charlestown: Samuel Etheridge, Jr., 1813.

Sloan, Douglas, *The Scottish Enlightenment and the American College Ideal,* New York: Teachers College Press, 1971.

Smith, Robert, *A Compleat System of Opticks: A Popular, a Mathematical, and a Philosophical Treastise,* Cambridge: Cornelius Crownfield, 1738.

Sommerville, D.M.Y., *Elements of Non-Euclidean Geometry,* London: G. Bell and Sons, Ltd., 1914.

Stewart, Dugald, *Collected Works*, Hamilton, William, ed., Edinburgh: T. & T. Clark, 1877.

Index